Education in Community Development

PRAEGER SPECIAL STUDIES IN
INTERNATIONAL ECONOMICS AND DEVELOPMENT

Education in Community Development

ITS FUNCTION IN TECHNICAL ASSISTANCE

James J. Shields, Jr.

FREDERICK A. PRAEGER, Publishers
New York · Washington · London

The purpose of the Praeger Special Studies is to make specialized research monographs in U.S. and international economics and politics available to the academic, business, and government communities. For further information, write to the Special Projects Division, Frederick A. Praeger, Publishers, 111 Fourth Avenue, New York, N.Y. 10003.

FREDERICK A. PRAEGER, PUBLISHERS
111 Fourth Avenue, New York, N.Y. 10003, U.S.A.
77-79 Charlotte Street, London W.1, England

Published in the United States of America in 1967
by Frederick A. Praeger, Inc., Publishers

Library of Congress Catalog Card Number: 66-26572

Printed in the United States of America

CONTENTS

Education in Community Development

INTRODUCTION

The phrases "rising expectations," "the silent revolution," and "the take-off stage" are frequently used in circles where developing nations are discussed. Aside from revealing a penchant for the catchword and the slogan, they partly describe a phenomenon unique in our generation which has been steadfastly tugging at our collective coatsleeves for attention. Clearer and more violent expressions of this phenomenon were exhibited in the revolution in Cuba, the uprisings in the Congo, and the trouble in Vietnam. These expressions, verbal and physical, are all latter-day examples of the new importance the inhabitants of small rural villages are assuming in all parts of the world.

These villagers, who comprise about 80 per cent of the world's total population, have achieved a new image in the eyes of the rest of the world. Their nations are no longer spoken of as underdeveloped, but as developing; the villagers themselves are no longer spoken of as natives, but as nationals; and they are no longer given charity, but technical assistance. There is change on all sides as thoughtful men seek to understand what is sometimes a threat and is always a challenge.

Awakened with a sense of what Goethe meant when he said: "There is nothing more frightful than ignorance in action"[1] and motivated by sentiments which spring from a growing awareness of today's world problems--one of which Jaime Bodet describes so effectively:

> If we want to live in a united world we cannot allow the most unjust of all frontiers to go on existing . . . the frontier that divides those who can read from those who cannot. We have terrible memories of concentration camps, but we sometimes forget that without prisons or barbed wire, more than 1,200 million men and women live in the implacable inner dungeon of ignorance.[2]

1

--the United States,through the Agency for International Development and its predecessor agencies, has developed a myriad of technical assistance programs for these "peoples in the huts and villages of half the world struggling to break the bonds of mass misery."[3]

This study is an analysis from an educational point of view of one of these programs: the Agency for International Development and its predecessor agencies' activities in the field of community development.[4]

THE NEED FOR THE STUDY

Numerous studies have been undertaken on the economic factors, the political aspects, and the cultural implications of community development, but to date there are few analytic or descriptive studies of the educational components of community development. Therefore, this study, in focusing upon the educational aspects of community development, represents a departure in emphasis and concern from the earlier studies of the role of technical assistance in community development.

One of the very few descriptive studies of the United States' efforts in international education was made for the Committee on Government Operations and was published in a report entitled Government Programs in International Education.[5] Significantly, this report, which is little more than an outline, points to the need for a far more intensive study of the actual operations and impact of the United States' programs in international education.

The report conclusively demonstrates that the United States government is in the business of international education in a big way. It points out that each of the executive departments and most of the independent agencies of the government are carrying out educational activities which span practically all nations and all geographical areas of the world.

This study, which deals with the role of education in community development programs of AID and its predecessor agencies, will be of immediate practical value to those working in the field of community development as well as to those with a special interest in international education.

THE PURPOSE OF THE STUDY

The purpose of this study is to describe the role of education in the programs supported by AID and its predecessor agencies in order to discern hitherto unrecognized facets of the role of international education in community development.

Over the years social scientists have come to appreciate the interdependence of formal education, literacy training, and fundamental education with community development. While each of these aspects does indeed tell a part of the story of the relationship of education to community development, individually and collectively, they fall far short of providing a complete picture of the role of education in community development.

This study proposes that there are additional educational dimensions. These can be found in the work of the community development adviser, the internal training programs for community development personnel, and the participant training programs provided in the United States and third countries as well as in the very meaning of community development, which by definition is an educational process.

The introductory chapters of this study consist of a short history and an analysis of the philosophy of community development supported by AID and the functions performed by community development personnel who work for the agency. The remaining chapters deal with a description of the major educational activities related to intergovernmental programs in community development. These activities include advisory assistance, the support of training programs in cooperating countries, and participant training in the United States and third countries.

A CAUTION AND AN EXPLANATION

While the very purpose of this study requires that education be the central theme, it is never argued that education is the single most important factor in community development. The basic thesis of the study is better represented by saying that although education is an integral and significant element in community development programs, it is only one of the many processes operative in any community development program.

Thus, this study, while complete in terms of what it sets out to do, is in no way a complete study of community development. A functioning community development program defies the demarcations carefully established by the separate disciplines and the subject areas. As a consequence, a complete exploration of the totality of processes involved in community development calls for the implementation of the knowledge and the tools of many fields. It calls, in fact, for an interdisciplinary study. Because of the nature of community development, any study which emphasizes one subject area or discipline is necessarily a partial study.

In the past, many looked to the sociologist for answers to the problems faced by community development workers; and, certainly, the word "community" itself suggests the relevance of this field. However, it is well to realize that no one field holds the key to all that is significant in community development. The sociologist, while traditionally an important figure in the field of community development, can no more claim the right to be principal spokesman and architect than can an agriculturist or an educationist.

It does not take too much reflection to discover the pertinence of many other academic disciplines to the study of community development. For instance, we find that an examination of the process of development, from the standpoint of local cultural patterns, of necessity involves the field of anthropology. The study of community development programs sponsored by a governmental agency involved in international affairs introduces the fields of international affairs and political science. We could easily add examples involving the fields of economics, industrial management, public administration, and social work.

Community development will not become an effective instrument until all the fields whose concerns touch on community development are recognized and utilized in planning, programing, and evaluation. Whenever community development becomes the exclusive domain of any one discipline or subject area, whether it is sociology, social work, or anthropology, it is doomed to one-sidedness and a severely limited range of success.

THE RESEARCH FOR THE STUDY

In 1961, the International Cooperation Administration, [6] which was a predecessor agency of AID, drafted a policy to allow university researchers to undertake historical research on its activities. Under this liberalized policy, the original research for this study was done in the spring and summer of 1961 and the final draft was completed in the summer of 1966 in the Department of State, Washington, D. C. Specifically, the study is based upon an examination of government files, published and unpublished reports, documents in the various libraries in the State Department, and interviews with agency administrators in Washington, D. C., and with staff members returning from overseas assignments.

For the most part, this study is based upon previously unavailable records of the experiences of the men and women in AID and its predecessor agencies who were involved in community development programs. In this sense, it constitutes a unique and a significant contribution to the fields of community development and international education.

However, there are also a number of clearly defined limits to the study. AID's records were studied and analyzed without the full benefit of knowing the field conditions under which they were written or of knowing the authors. Also, the research was based upon information secured mainly through AID. Other government agencies and other organizations working in the field of community development were not consulted. For these reasons, no attempt is made to evaluate AID and its predecessor agencies or to compose a list of recommendations for the field of community development in general. Instead, the main purposes of the study are the provision of a sketch of AID's activities in community development and an analysis of the role of education in these activities.

The Washington staff of AID, particularly those who have administrative responsibility for community development, were extremely helpful and offered a number of important suggestions which were incorporated into the final draft. The background they provided on the conditions and problems faced by the overseas staff was especially valuable in placing the records used for this study in proper perspective.

A special word of appreciation is owed to E. Gordon Alderfer, C. David Anderson, John Bright, Lucy Brown, Barbara Doyle, Frances Howard, John Kenny, Robert McMillan, Louis Miniclier, Charles Minor, Carol Piper, Henrietta Villaescusa, and all of the AID staff who gave so generously of their time to answer the innumerable questions I had about the work of AID in the field of community development and who did so much to make my research in Washington efficient and pleasant.

NOTES TO INTRODUCTION

[1]Cited by Mark Van Doren, Man's Right to Knowledge and the Free Use Thereof (New York: Columbia University, 1954), p. 12.

[2]United Nations Educational, Scientific and Cultural Organization, Learn and Live, Foreword by Jaime T. Bodet (Paris: UNESCO, 1951), Foreword.

[3]John F. Kennedy,"Inaugural Address, " The New York Times, January 22, 1961, p. 8.

[4]Throughout the rest of the study the initials AID will be used in place of Agency for International Development.

[5]United States Congress, House Committee on Government Operations, Government Programs in International Education (Washington, D. C.: Government Printing Office, 1959), p. 6.

[6]Throughout the rest of the study the initials ICA will be used in place of International Cooperation Administration.

CHAPTER 1

A PERSPECTIVE ON
THE COMMUNITY
DEVELOPMENT
ACTIVITIES OF AID

THE AID[1]

AID performs its functions as an agency within the Department of State. The director of the agency reports directly to the Secretary of State and the President and is charged with central direction and responsibility for the economic assistance program and for the coordination of the military and economic assistance programs.

The organization structure of the agency consists of the Office of the Administrator, four regional bureaus to carry out the program, program offices and staffs to assist the administrator in dealing with broad functional areas and international programs, offices to assist the administrator in managing the affairs of the agency, and missions overseas which develop the programs of assistance in cooperation with the government of the participating country and work closely with the local officials in program execution.

The regional bureaus have the responsibility for program planning and the execution of United States economic development programs overseas. The line of responsibility runs directly from the chief administrator through the directors of the regional bureaus to the ambassadors and then on to the directors of AID missions overseas.

United States assistance activities to developing nations take a variety of forms. Some of the important development assistance tools used are development loans, development grants and technical cooperation, supporting assistance, and the contingency fund. Development loans constitute the major share of AID assistance, and the proportion of loans to total assistance has grown steadily over the past few years. Nearly 60 per cent of the total economic assistance program funds spent in 1966, for instance, were development loans, including loans to Latin American countries under the

Alliance for Progress.

Development loans are intended for high-priority capital projects which either directly produce revenue or are important to the economic infrastructure of a country. These include establishing or expanding manufacturing facilities, development banks, irrigation power, multipurpose water resource development, mining, ports, and grain storage facilities. Loan funds are available also for programs and projects designed to promote social development, including schools, hospitals, and housing, as well as for programs in areas such as adult education and community development.

Development grants are used to promote the economic development of less developed friendly countries and areas, with emphasis on assisting the development of human resources through such means as programs of technical cooperation. Much of the development grant and technical cooperation program is directed to training needed specialists, technicians, professionals, and administrators in less developed countries by sending abroad American specialists and advisers, or by bringing trainees to the United States or to other developed countries.

During the last decade of United States official technical assistance programs, it has become clear that transferring skills through demonstration and training must be supplemented by developing the institutions and organizations needed to make trained people effective. Thus, development grant and technical cooperation activities are also directed to building a wide variety of institutions, including school systems and universities, agricultural extension services, public health systems, trade and credit associations, labor unions, and cooperatives.

Development grant funds are also used to finance surveys, research, and analysis of development needs. Finally, development grant funds finance projects and contribute directly to improved health, housing, or other areas of public welfare; for example, malaria eradication projects.

Supporting assistance is normally used to further urgent United States national security and foreign policy objectives where the usual criteria for development loans or grants cannot be met. Normally, it is used for the following purposes:

(a) to enable countries to make a greater contribution to the common defense, or to internal security, than their economies can support; (b) to maintain economic stability in countries where the absence or drastic reduction of current support would probably involve disastrous economic and political disintegration; and (c) to provide an alternative to Sino-Soviet Bloc aid, where such aid threatens a country's independence or otherwise conflicts with vital United States interests.

The contingency fund is an emergency reserve fund for meeting urgent and unforeseen requirements for economic assistance. It has been used to meet needs which have resulted from earthquakes, floods, military actions, or for meeting requirements that cannot be clearly defined or accurately costed in advance. The fund is used for both developmental and supporting assistance activities.

Technical Cooperation

The best publicized and, consequently, the most widely known aspect of AID's work is its technical cooperation program. Programs in health, labor, agriculture, and community development all fall under this general heading. While technical cooperation is well known, it is rarely understood. This is because its emphasis is totally different from that of any other activity. The focus is always upon human resources. It is necessarily a person-to-person activity, which deals primarily with the development of people. Material development, while not neglected, is given secondary consideration.

The early postwar economic assistance efforts in Europe under the Marshall Plan provided a historical precedent for large-scale aid programs. However, they did not provide a precedent for the type of aid needed by the developing nations of Africa, Asia, and Latin America in the 1950's and 1960's. The great need in Western Europe after the war was for physical resources. For the most part, Western Europe had the basic institutions and trained manpower. On the other hand, the need in developing nations is quite different. Their need for new institutions and for trained manpower is so great that the need for capital is often secondary. This new need was a major factor in shaping AID's philosophy of technical cooperation. [2]

Technical cooperation operates on the premise that

when people develop other forms of development follow. The materials of technical cooperation are skills, knowledge and attitudes, and the relatively small amounts of supplies and equipment required for demonstration purposes.

Technical cooperation is not a new concept. It has existed for as long as men have shared their technical knowledge and skills with other men. The first man to demonstrate the use of the wheel to his neighbors was in a very real sense involved in a venture in technical cooperation. As man systematically organized the sharing of technical knowledge on a wide scale, the concept of a technical cooperation program emerged. Basically, technical cooperation programs function to bring the proven skills and techniques of the advanced nations to the people of the less developed areas of the world.

Precedents for AID

President Truman, in the fourth point of his Inaugural Address, proposed a program for helping people in under-developed areas to help themselves. This program, named "Point Four" by the press, has become as famous in the history of American foreign policy as the Monroe Doctrine. The address contained the basic philosophy of technical assistance which is still used as a guide for present-day aid programs.

President Truman's statement on technical assistance led to the passage of the International Development of the Foreign Economic Assistance Act of 1950, which was the establishing act of the Technical Cooperation Administration of the Department of State, an agency created to administer technical assistance in underdeveloped areas. The Technical Cooperation Administration was preceded by two other agencies, both of which carried on technical assistance programs. The first was the Institute of Inter-American Affairs, which grew out of the Buenos Aires Convention of 1938 and became the operating agency for technical assistance programs in Latin America. The other was the agency which handled economic assistance programs in Europe, the Economic Cooperation Administration, established in 1948 under the Foreign Assistance Act.

These separate technical assistance programs continued very much as they were created until 1951, when an independent government agency, the Mutual Security Administration, absorbed the functions of the Economic Cooperation Administration. The next big change occurred in 1953. At that time, the Foreign Operations Administration was established in order to bring into a single organization the foreign assistance and the related economic operations formerly distributed among several agencies. As a result, the Technical Cooperation Administration, the Mutual Security Administration, and the Institute of Inter-American Affairs were all dissolved; and their separate functions were placed in one agency.

The spread of community development from India to other countries influenced the Foreign Operations Administration to establish a Community Development Division in the agency in 1954. The purpose of the division was (a) to serve as a focal point for community development on a worldwide basis, (b) to develop guidance material for United States missions overseas, (c) to participate in the review of country community development programs, (d) to assist with the development of training materials, (e) to assist with the recruiting and orientation of United States personnel, (f) to assist with the development of training programs for participants coming to the United States, and (g) to assist with the planning and coordination of United States government and voluntary agency community development activities. Up until this time, United States technical assistance activities in the field of community development had been administered by several divisions whose primary responsibilities were in areas other than community development.

On May 9, 1955, the International Cooperation Administration was established as a semiautonomous agency within the Department of State; and the functions formerly held by the Foreign Operations Administration were transferred to it. Until 1955, the operations of the agencies responsible for technical assistance were considered temporary. The placement of the general responsibility for operations and policy within the Department of State was considered by many as an indication that ICA would have a more secure position as a governmental agency than its predecessors had had. [3]

In 1961, the Foreign Assistance Act was passed by Congress. Soon after the passage of this act, the functions of ICA were absorbed into the newly created Agency for

International Development. As a result of this change, the Community Development Division was dissolved; and the importance of community development in United States technical cooperation programs declined.

The Act for International Development of 1961 emphasized the long-term nature of the development process and of development assistance, the importance of self-help, and the need for the concentration of aid, both among countries and upon selected sectors or areas of activity in each country. To incorporate these new emphases into the country assistance programs, new programing procedures and guidelines were developed and were applied to programs. These included longer-range planning, closer integration of assistance activities with United States foreign policy, closer integration of United States programs with those of other free-world donors, and closer integration of United States aid with the recipient country's development program. [4]

COMMUNITY DEVELOPMENT ACTIVITIES OF AID
AND ITS PREDECESSOR AGENCIES

Men, from the earliest periods of human history, have banded together to seek in common the development of their communities. Thus, while the term "community development" is relatively new, the principle behind it is almost as old as human communities. The term "community development" first achieved prominence at a conference held in Cambridge, England, in 1948, where it was introduced to describe a movement "to promote better living for the whole community on the initiative of the community."[5] Although the conference did not propose to encourage the widespread use of the term, within a short time the term "community development" replaced terms such as "mass education," "rural development," "community education," and "village development."

A Definition of Community Development

Efforts to define the United States' concept of community development were made shortly after a separate Community Development Division was established within ICA. On October 27, 1956, a four-page document entitled "The Community development Guidelines of the International Cooperation Administration"[6] was published and distributed to all United States Operations Missions.

This document defines community development as a method by which national governments reach out to people on the village level and help them use local initiative and resources to achieve increased production and higher standards of living and as a social process by which the people of a community define, solve, and actually work out, as a community, the problems they face, relying as much as they possibly can upon local resources. This definition is based on the premise that when people are given a chance to work out their own problems they will find solutions that have a lasting effect.[7] The core concept is self-help.

Within the terms of this definition, physical improvements within a community are not as important as the changes which take place within people. Thus, the emphasis is not placed upon road building, agricultural quotas, or the number of wells to be dug, but upon group discussion, democratic organization, and the techniques needed to involve large numbers of people actively in discussion and action. Community development is presented as a means for achieving a unified approach to village improvement by increasing local skill in the use of the democratic processes.

The "Guidelines" move on from a statement of the philosophy of community development to a discussion of organizational patterns. No one organizational pattern is recommended as suitable; instead, flexibility is suggested. It is pointed out that, because the availability of money and the attitudes of government officials differ from country to country, different organizational patterns must be used.

The "Guidelines" stress the importance of highly coordinated programs. There is no sign of flexibility in the demand for this factor. Coordination, the "Guidelines" suggest, is best achieved when a community development program has the support of the highest officers in the government, has a corps of multipurpose workers, has the support of the technical ministries, and has training centers for community development personnel.[8]

The "Guidelines" contain in one form or another the principles of national support, the training of community development workers at all levels, the use of multipurpose workers, the self-help concept, and the commitment to democratic values and processes. In the years that followed,

each of these principles emerged as major identifying characteristics of the philosophy of community development
supported by AID and its predecessor agencies.

The United States brought five years of international
experience in the field of community development to the task
of formulating the "Guidelines." Thus, it is not at all sur-
prising to discover that in 1966, ten years after the "Guidelines" were written, they still represent the best statement
available on the agency's philosophy. Easily, the "Guidelines"
is the most important document the agency has published on
community development. The principles it contains are
briefly stated, yet general enough that they have applicability
to a wide range of cultures and concise enough that they
should prove to be a meaningful guide for those interested in
establishing effective community development programs anywhere in the world.

In the ten-year period between 1952 and 1962, the
United States spent approximately $50 million in support of
community development through its foreign assistance program. Almost one half of this amount was spent to establish
major programs in India, Pakistan, and the Philippines.
Prior to 1955, United States assistance for community development emphasized equipment and supplies, such as vehicles for village workers. Since 1955, the emphasis has
shifted to providing technicians and participant training, plus
small amounts of supplies and equipment. [9] What follows is
a capsule statement on the programs in India, Pakistan, and
the Philippines.

The First National Program

If any moment can be singled out as the most significant
in the history of United States activities in the area of intergovernmental programs in community development, it would
be the signing of the joint agreement in 1952, which continued
until 1959, between the United States and India establishing
India's community development program.

The signing of this agreement provided the United
States with the protracted experience in a full-scale national
program that it required to build a comprehensive philosophy
of community development appropriate for use in underdeveloped nations.

The Indian program did not begin United States participation in intergovernmental programs in community development. Prior to the major development in India which launched the community development idea on a national scale, the Technical Cooperation Mission in Jordan and Iran contracted with the Near East Foundation to undertake community improvement work on a pilot scale in a series of villages in both these countries.

The Near East Foundation program was essentially a publicly supported program of sending social workers into village areas to train local people in leadership roles and then applying the training and leadership to local situations which the people of the village felt were important to them. These efforts usually started with a school, a small health clinic, or an agricultural program of some kind; and eventually the whole village area was enveloped or involved in some sort of development program. [10]

The American technicians who went to India in the early days were encouraged by the success of India's program to change their concept of community development from one which concentrated upon the establishment of a series of small isolated programs to a concept which embraced a broad national program.

United States aid enabled India to inaugurate the first national community development program in the world on Mahatma Gandhi's birthday, October 2, 1952. The United States provided approximately $8.5 million of financial aid and technical assistance, mostly in the form of specialists in agriculture, education, vocational training, and extension procedures. These specialists assisted at every level of the program at training centers, on the State Development Commissioner's staff, in the technical agencies which served the community development program, and in the National Extension Service.

The success of India's program demonstrated that the preconditions necessary for economic growth can be established at the same time democratic institutions are being strengthened. This success was a convincing revelation to those who doubted that rapid economic growth could take place within the framework of democracy. While the physical accomplishments of the program were astounding, they were not nearly as impressive as the strides that were made in building the foundations of a democratic society.

However, as time went on, a number of observers reported that the Indian program tended to emphasize agricultural production to the virtual exclusion of other goals. [11] They found that this tendency undermined many of India's earlier gains in the areas of civic responsibilities and democratic values. Also, it was found that many Indians approached the program with an eye to how much they could personally profit rather than with a spirit of giving. [12] These factors, many observers felt, resulted in the lessening of the significance of India's program, which for many years served as the greatest experiment in a nationally supported community development program in the world.

The Agreement with Pakistan

In the summer of 1952, the United States entered into an agreement with Pakistan to help institute a national community development program. Under this agreement, the United States sent technicians who were specialists in agriculture, health, cottage industries, adult literacy, communications, home economics, and housing to provide advisory assistance at various governmental levels and at the training institutes. In addition, a number of Pakistani nationals were selected for training in the United States and third countries; and material aid was given in the form of transportation equipment and training aids.

The Village-AID program, the name given to community development activities in Pakistan, was evaluated a number of times by visiting teams from the executive and legislative branches of the United States Government. All the teams concluded that Pakistan was making substantial progress in achieving its objectives in the field of community development. [13]

Nonetheless, the Village-AID program was abolished in Pakistan in 1959. According to Ernest Neal, the opponents of the program claimed that it had bypassed existing administrative machinery and established a new administrative organization for community development. It was also claimed that the paid village-level workers became identified with the large farm owners who did not work with the soil. Unfortunately, the tenants who worked the land were not enthusiastic about improved practices because most of the increased

COMMUNITY DEVELOPMENT ACTIVITIES OF AID 17

production went to the landlord. A program named Basic Democracies was established to overcome the shortcomings of the Village-AID program. In 1961, shortly after the creation of the Basic Democracies program, the United States discontinued its assistance to Pakistan. [14]

Mr. Sol D. Ozer of the AID Mission in Pakistan, who has observed the Basic Democracies in action, states:

Something unusual and unanticipated by its fondest advocates has come to pass. In a surprisingly short time, the Basic Democracies took hold. Its roots are in the people in the villages and the people believed and responded. A technique that was designed to better government and direct the people has in fact turned out to be a channel through which the people are challenging those who have been elected to govern them. [15]

The Philippine Program

Previous to 1956, India's community development program and, to a much lesser degree, the Pakistani program were the two largest and most effective programs supported by American technical assistance funds. In 1956, the United States agreed to assist the Philippine Government to establish a countrywide community development program. Within a very short period, the Philippine program surpassed both the Indian and Pakistani programs in effectiveness and stature.

The work of a rural sociologist who was employed by the United States Operations Mission (USOM) in the Philippines for over four years was mainly responsible for the interest of the Philippine Government in community development. During this period, he assisted the Philippine Government in planning and carrying out pilot projects.

The success of these projects and President Magsaysay's conviction that community development represented the best means available to raise the standard of living of the peasants in the barrios led the President of the Philippines to request the United States to help him to initiate a nationwide community development program. In answer to this request, the United States agreed to provide technical assistance.

The Philippine community development program generally adhered to the specific objective of encouraging the actual
growth of local village organizations. At no time were the
program's goals defined purely in terms of providing the
government with a vehicle for the districution of services,
supplies, and credit. Neither was the program seen as an
administrative arm of the government for law, order, finance,
or administration.

The program developed rapidly. In less than a year, nine
training centers for community development workers were established; and 158 workers were carrying on pilot projects in
twenty-two provinces scattered over fifty municipalities.
The progress continued in the years that followed. Between
1957 and 1963, upwards of 40, 814 self-help projects were
initiated, of which about 85 per cent were completed. Over
this period, training was provided for 1, 262 workers, 700
of whom were serving in 5, 231 barrios. In addition to training
its own people, the Philippine Government by 1959 provided
training for 700 community development specialists from
other nations, primarily in South Asia and the Far East.

The record in terms of changed attitudes and local
autonomy is even more impressive. In one year alone, 1958-
59, the number of elected barrios increased from 6, 000 to
12, 000. This led to the enactment of a new barrio autonomy
law which became effective on January 1, 1960. As a direct
result of this law, democratically elected village governments
were given the legal authority to improve the conditions of
barrio life. [16]

Carlos P. Garcia, President of the Philippines, in a
speech at Cagayan de Oro on May 30, 1960, described the
success of the community development program in the Philippines:

> . . . (the Philippine community development pro-
> gram) is succeeding in bringing about a perceptible
> change in the attitudes of our people from one of
> dependence on government to self-reliance and
> thus helping to create a rural citizenry that is
> alert, dynamic, responsive, and self-reliant. [17]

In spite of this record of success, in 1966 the United
States wrote an end to the ten-year partnership with the

Philippine Government which resulted in the creation and evolution of the Presidential Assistant on Community Development (PACD) into one of the ablest agencies for national progress in the world. AID's rationale for phasing out the assistance program was that while some purposes were realized, others, such as increased productivity and income of the barrio people and the better coordination of government services, had not been achieved on a nationwide basis. [18]

Basically, AID withdrew because as an agency it has become more and more preoccupied with quantitative results. Unfortunately, increased social participation and political development, which are major products of community development, are hard to measure. This explains why the support of community development as an instrument of United States foreign policy has decreased in importance within AID.

Also, AID is impelled to focus upon agricultural production in the face of projected world starvation within fifteen years. Thus, the agency is dropping community development in favor of rural development, which it considers to be a more effective means of resolving the food problem. In so doing, the agency has reasoned that community development has served its purpose by helping stem the spread of Communism in India and the Philippines by laying the foundations for local autonomy in these nations.

The Philippines reacted strongly to AID's withdrawal of support of its nation's community development program in favor of rural development. The Philippine Government is determined to carry forward its well-established community development effort in both rural and urban areas with increased help from the United States Peace Corps and other volunteer groups.

African Programs [19]

Current United States technical assistance activities reflect a deep interest in community development on the part of African nations. In several countries there is evidence of increasing support on the part of governments in initiating or expanding community development programs as part of their nation-building efforts. In 1966, AID assisted six countries to develop and expand programs. These countries are Kenya, Malawi, Sierra Leone, Tanzania, Togoland, and Zambia.

The major focus in programs supported by AID in Africa is upon the development of institutions to provide the trained personnel required for local dissemination of the objectives and techniques of community development. This includes the establishment of a program requiring trained staff, curricula, and the development and the publication of training materials suitable for training community-level staff.

A short description of the Kenyan and the Tanzanian projects provides good insight into the direction the African programs are moving. In Kenya, a project was initiated in 1961 to train a cadre of community development personnel and to establish a string of training institutes. Following independence and the decision of the government of Kenya to develop a national plan for community development, two other elements were added: local leadership training at district centers and pilot demonstration projects. In 1964, a fourth activity, research and evaluation, was added. To date, a total of 217 community development staff members have been trained in Kenya and are now employed at national, district, and local levels. Of these, eleven were trained in a two-year professional course, the first to be given in Africa.

In Tanzania, the government has geared its program into political development, reaching from the center down to the village level. A system of development committees at village, district, and regional levels is used to relate projects at the community level to the over-all development plans of the nation. Here, as in Kenya, AID assistance is focused primarily upon training.

Latin American Programs

Latin Americans are looking more and more to community development as an answer to their development problems. At the moment, community development programs play an extremely small role in the total development picture; but all signs point to rapid expansion of these programs in the not too distant future.

An interesting feature of some of the Latin American programs is the use of community development to meet urban problems. In Brazil, for instance, an urban community development program has been initiated in Rio in the form of pilot projects in selected slum areas. The program is to be expanded later to an area in southern Brazil and an area in the northeast. It involves the short-term, low-skill level, vocational training of young adults, job placement, and aided self-help projects designed to improve living conditions and create new sources of income.

Efforts are being made to establish large-scale national community development programs in Bolivia, Guatamala, and Peru with AID assistance. In Bolivia, an AID community development adviser has been working with Bolivian officials, the Peace Corps, and Cornell University advisers to formulate a national community development program aimed at Indian integration and involving the coordination of technical services in rural areas. Although not much beyond the launching stage, the program has had a large measure of success and shows promise of becoming one of the most successful national programs in Latin America.

In Guatamala, a new national community development program has been undertaken by the government with technical assistance from AID. It is anticipated that AID will assist the effort further through loans, grants, and the provision of a community development advisory staff. The program seeks to strengthen the capacities of local governments to support self-help programs.

A major national community development effort is "Cooperacion Popular" in Peru initiated by President Balaunde to involve restive rural masses in local development. The program is designed to provide newly elected units of government with the means for undertaking aided self-help projects. AID has assisted this program by providing technical assistance in its formulation and initiation. There are three community development advisers, with a fourth administering a grant-in-aid program to local communities, on the staff of the United States Mission in Peru. AID has also provided grants and commodities of approximately $600,000.

The United States also assists community development efforts in Chile, the Dominican Republic, Ecuador, El Salvador, Honduras, Mexico, Panama, and Venezuela.

UNITED STATES CONTRIBUTIONS TO THE FIELD OF COMMUNITY DEVELOPMENT

The United States Government supported community

development at a crucial time in world history. Shortly after
the Second World War, the problems of tyranny, disease,
hunger, and ignorance became grave international concerns.
The implications of problems of this nature passed through
more men's minds and touched more men's hearts than ever
before in the history of mankind. Answers were sought, and
nations were willing to institute new and radical programs to
solve these problems. India, Pakistan, Iran, and Nepal saw
an answer in community development. However, this solution required more money and greater numbers of skilled
technicians than these countries had at their disposal.

The United States, recognizing the need and the time-
liness of the concept, provided the aid necessary to implement broad-scale community development programs in India
and Pakistan and a number of other newly independent and
developing nations. Community development could not have
attained the stature it has attained if support had not been
given by the United States at this time.

Second, the United States helped synthesize into a
unified concept the many scattered ideas held about community development. The ideas the United States supported
were not at all original. They were culled from the experiences of numerous community development workers who had
carried on a series of national and international programs
over the years. However, it was not until 1952, when India
established her program with the support of the United States,
that these ideas were combined into a large national program.
The ideas India and the United States worked out at this time
became the basis for the principles set forth in the "Guidelines"
composed by ICA staff members in 1956 and the philosophy
of community development supported by the United States
today.

In effect, the Indian program was a watershed in which
the most appropriate of the old ideas were fused with new
ideas as they emerged. The United States, through its position in the Indian program, was able to play a significant role
in the synthesis of the old and the new principles of community development into a viable concept.

Third, the United States has helped establish community
development as an important international movement. Each
year community development has attracted the attention of

more and more people from all over the world. All in all,
over forty countries, including Canada and several European
countries, but especially the less developed nations, are
involved in community development programs. This was not
always the case.Less than twenty years ago community development was no more than a series of isolated programs in a
few countries scattered around the world. Now, it is a self-
conscious movement on an international level. The effects
of this new internationalism in community development can
be found throughout the world. India, for instance, sent an
adviser to Ethiopia and strongly supported the program in
Nepal. The Philippines has opened her training program to
visitors from other nations. And observers from Ghana
visited India, Koreans visited Iran, and Brazilians visited
Puerto Rico. [20]

The United States has figured prominently in this
growth through the provision of funds for participant training
in the United States and third countries, conferences and
seminars, publications, the exchange of United States technicians, and the sponsorship of teams to evaluate community
development programs. These and other techniques have
done much to contribute to the growing belief that community
development is a world movement.

Finally, the United States has supplemented the efforts
of other international organizations in establishing community
development as a potent weapon in man's battle against ignorance, hunger, and disease. The success of the programs
in the Philippines and India, both of which were supported by
the United States, provides statistical evidence for maintaining that community development is a worthy armament in
man's oldest and most elemental battle--the battle against
hunger, tyranny, disease, and ignorance.

CONCLUSION

In the light of these contributions, it is unfortunate that
community development as an instrument of national development is losing the support of many high-ranking AID policy-
makers. They mistakenly believe that community development is concerned with fringe activities and that it contrib-
utes little to the economic development of the nations aided.

A major contributing factor to the diminishing role

being assigned community development in United States technical assistance activities is the active position maintained
by development economists within AID.   They recommend
that no funds be expended on so-called amenities for subsistence farmers.   They believe that the limited funds available for development should be spent on the small class of
commercial farmers who can produce with improved technology enough food to support a nation.

However, as Ernest Neal points out, if the views of
these development economists are implemented, then all
development funds will be spent on approximately 20 per cent
of the population who are commercial farmers and on urban
workers who hold industrial positions.   When this happens, a
political situation will be precipitated among subsistence
agricultural groups which can threaten the stability of the
nation.   The governments of developing nations cannot, nor
can the United States Government, afford to ignore the political significance of the subsistence peasant farmer.   Political
facts of life indicate that a share of the development funds
must be directed toward improving the lot of subsistence
peasants.   And this is where community development has
proven itself an effective tool for national development.[21]
By definition, community development is geared to incorpo-
rating all the people, but especially the disadvantaged, into
the total life of a nation.

This opposition within AID does not mean that community development is a dead item on the technical assistance
agenda.   As indicated in this chapter, there are still a large
number of community development programs actively supported by the United States.   The chapters that follow deal,
for the most part, with the principles implemented by those
within AID who are responsible for staffing AID activities in
the field of community development.

NOTES TO CHAPTER 1

[1]The material in this section is based upon the following sources: United States General Services Administration, National Archives and Records Section, United States Government Organization Manual, 1965-1966 (Washington, D.C.: Government Printing Office, n.d.), pp. 90-92; and United States AID, Principles of Foreign Economic Assistance (Washington, D.C.: Government Printing Office, 1965), pp. 14-15, 18-21.

[2]United States Department of State, et al., The Mutual Security Program, Fiscal Year 1951, A Summary Presentation (Washington, D.C.: Government Printing Office, 1960), pp. 16, 46-53.

[3]United States Congress, House Committee on Government Operations, Government Programs in International Education (Washington, D.C.: Government Printing Office, 1959), p. 38.

[4]United States AID, op. cit., pp. 10-11.

[5]Irwin T. Sanders, Community Development and National Change (Washington, D.C.: Community Development Division, ICA, 1958), p. 3.

[6]United States ICA, Community Development Division, "The Community Development Guidelines of the International Cooperation Administration" (Washington, D.C.: The Division, ICA, 1956), p. 4.

[7]Ibid., p. 1.

[8]Ibid., p. 2.

[9]Cited by Ernest Neal in A Report to the Assistant Administrator for Technical Cooperation and Research in the Agency for International Development Program of Community Development (Washington, D.C.: AID, 1964), p. 18.

[10] Stanley Andrews, A Comment and Review of Community Development Projects (Washington, D. C.: Technical Assistance Study Group, ICA, 1961), p. 4.

[11] Ernest Neal, "The Community Development Approach to Economic Development and Democratic Government in Underdeveloped Areas" (Manila: ICA, 1957), p. 23.

[12] United Nations, Bureau of Social Affairs, International Survey of Programs of Social Development (New York: United Nations, 1959), p. 157.

[13] James W. Green, "Rural Development in Pakistan: The Village Aid Program" (Washington, D. C.: Community Development Division, ICA, n. d.), pp. 6–7, 12, 22.

[14] Ernest Neal, "A Report on Community Development in the Philippines, East Pakistan and India" (Washington, D. C.: AID, 1964), p. 12.

[15] Ibid., p. 7.

[16] R. V. Bernhart, et al., letters, memoranda, and reports. Copies found in the country file under "Philippines 1960," Community Development Division, ICA, Washington, D. C.

[17] Carlos P. Garcia, speech at Cagayan de Oro, May 30, 1960. Copy found in country file under "Philippines 1960," Community Development Division, ICA, Washington, D. C.

[18] Exequiel Molina, "PACD–AID Estrangement Calls for a Long Hard Look at Rural Development, "The Economic Monitor (Manila, May 16, 1966), p.8.

[19] Louis Miniclier, "AID Community Development in Africa" (Washington, D. C.: AID, 1965), pp. 1-2.

[20] United States ICA, Community Development Division, "Community Development Conference, Seoul, Korea, May 6–12, 1961, Briefing and Background for Senior Representative of the United States" (Washington, D. C.: The Division, ICA, 1961), unnumbered.

[21]Ernest Neal, A Report to the Assistant Administrator for Technical Cooperation and Research on the Agency for International Development Program of Community Development Assistance, op. cit., pp. 38-39.

CHAPTER **2**

THE GUIDING PRIN-
CIPLES OF UNITED
STATES TECHNICAL
ASSISTANCE ACTIVITIES
IN THE FIELD OF COM-
MUNITY DEVELOPMENT

There is a discernible consistency in the philosophy of community development supported, encouraged, and stimulated by AID and its predecessor agencies. Over the years, United States overseas technicians in the field of community development have attempted to develop programs which are characterized by (1) national support, (2) a corps of multipurpose workers, (3) extensive training programs, (4) political as well as economic goals, (5) a research and evaluation program, and (6) the self-help principle.

United States support of these particular elements was largely determined by two factors in the early history of its involvement in community development activities overseas. When the United States first entered the field of community development on an international scale, it recruited most of its technicians for overseas work from the discipline of rural sociology. As a result, many of the ideas associated with rural sociology were incorporated into its programs. These included training programs, political as well as economic goals, the self-help principle, and research and evaluation activities.

The other factor which shaped United States thinking was its early support and active participation in India's community development program. United States participation in this program added the principles of national support and the multipurpose worker to its basic concept of community development. Historically, the influence of American rural sociologists and India's community development program are the two most important factors in shaping United States thinking regarding overseas community development programs.

Although the United States has not been able to implement these principles in all the countries it has helped, nonetheless it has been constant in its support of them in its directives and in the literature it publishes on community development. As early as 1953, the Community Services

Staff of the Technical Cooperation Administration, one of the predecessor agencies of the AID, outlined a number of these principles in a paper entitled "Methods of Obtaining Community Participation in Self-help Activities. "[1] In January, 1961, the same principles were reflected in the conclusions of a SEATO Conference on Community Development sponsored by the United States. [2] These two documents, spanning almost a decade, signify the continuous support the United States has given to these principles.

Many of these principles can also be identified in one form or another with earlier programs of the British, the United Nations, and the Ford Foundation. For example, the British emphasized the effectiveness of using community development to achieve political purposes; and the United Nations stressed the importance of training all levels of personnel.

Therefore, the concept of community development supported by AID and its predecessor agencies represents a synthesis of many ideas which had been implemented in one area of the world or another long before the United States adopted them. Within this context, the major contribution of the United States is that of a synthesizer who has given these principles added strength through a wide range of international activities.

NATIONAL SUPPORT

The principle of national support for community development programs came into its own with the initiation of India's program in 1952. At that time, there were no precedents for it in either America or Europe. The principle is mainly an outgrowth of the surging nationalism which swept through India and many of the other developing nations after World War II.

The record of success in those countries with strong national support for their community development programs and of relative failure in those countries that do not have this kind of support has convinced the United States of the soundness of this principle.

The United States has found that strong national support is a significant factor in the success of the community development programs in India and the Philippines. It is more than a coincidence that the two countries with the most successful programs are those with the strongest national support. Carl Taylor, in speaking of India's program, singled out the Prime Minister's public approval of the program and the power it received through the Prime Minister's personal assumption of the chairmanship of the community development commission as major factors in determining its success. [3]

There is a similar pattern in the Philippines. President Magsaysay, shortly after becoming President, instituted a national community development program and gave it personal and constant support. He demonstrated the seriousness of his intention to make the program work by creating a special office of Presidential Assistant on Community Development (PACD).

The United States has found that strong nationally supported community development programs are valuable for a number of reasons. First, changes sought on the village level usually require far-reaching institutional changes beyond the village. For instance, problems of land tenure, usury, and corrupt government necessitate changes on provincial and national levels as well as on the local level.

Second, the avowed purpose of those establishing community development programs is to incorporate village communities into the life of the nation. [4] This cannot be achieved until governments on the national level institute philosophical and administrative changes.

A strong nationally supported community development program provides the ideal way for giving the rural populations a role in national politics. The purpose of community development is to create a bridge between the central authorities and local practices which will enable local citizens to express their needs in a political process that is directly related to the sphere of national decision making. [5] This is achieved only in programs that have strong national support. If village reform is to be achieved, links have to be created between the local citizen, the village as a community, and the national government. Each element has a significant role to play in determining the success or the failure of local and national change.

Third, community development calls for an integrated rather than a fragmented provision of technical services on the local level. This integration is achieved through the multipurpose worker. For the most part, multipurpose workers who carry out community development programs on the village level have limited technical skills and, therefore, need the assistance of technical specialists. The multipurpose worker in this role becomes the coordinator of the ordering and the supply of technical services provided to people on the village level. His job is to see that the village is given technical assistance at a rate which is consistent with its needs and its ability to accept it.

This calls for the cooperation and the support of technical divisions which traditionally mistrust and, more often than not, oppose the community development movement. A closer coordination of services can be achieved if the ministries and the departments working through the multipurpose workers are oriented toward the community development approach. Most importantly, it can be achieved if an attempt is made to coordinate the programs of the technical departments at all administrative levels, but especially on the national level.

The United States has found that these objectives are achieved most easily where ministries for community development have a director with high governmental status. This institutionalizes the formulation of policies from the highest level of the government all the way down to the village. It also builds into the system the authority needed to require the heads of national departments and agencies to coordinate their services in the field. [6]

THE MULTIPURPOSE VILLAGE-LEVEL WORKER

In the final analysis, the real test of the success of the programs supported by AID and its predecessor agencies is their operational effectiveness on the village level. The provision of adequate personnel for village-level work poses problems wherever community development programs are attempted. India, for reasons of economy and program integration, solved the problem by developing a civil servant unique to the underdeveloped countries--the paid multipurpose village worker. A popular way of providing technical assistance on the village level up until this time had been through

the team approach, which was widely supported by the British
and UNESCO. At a conference for community development
specialists, Margaret Read pointed out that the concept of a
multipurpose worker was not taught in British training
schools for community development workers before 1952,
when India introduced the idea.[7]

Traditionally, a team was composed of a number of
technicians, each representing a different field. There were
usually technicians from the fields of health, agriculture,
education, and frequently someone who specialized in cottage
industries, recreation, public administration, or road building. Each technician worked with the villagers in terms of
his own specialty. Each member of the team had a specialized function, whereas the multipurpose worker, who receives rudimentary training in a wide range of technical
skills, works with villagers on all of their problems regard-
less of the technical field involved.

Some predicted that the multipurpose worker would replace the technical specialists in the field. However, this
has not proven to be the case at all. Not only do technicians
continue to be as important as ever, but their positions are
enhanced. The multipurpose worker stimulates the villagers
to want technical assistance, prepares them to fully utilize
the assistance they receive, and follows up the technicians'
advice with supplementary help and encouragement. In addition, the multipurpose worker performs many routine and
elementary technical assistance functions which frees the
technician for more important assistance activities.

Ideally, technical specialists and multipurpose workers
are partners in a cooperative venture to develop village communities. Unfortunately, they are not always able to define
their roles clearly enough to avoid friction and misunderstanding. However, this does not provide sufficient grounds
to call the entire concept of the multipurpose worker into
question as many do. It may mean that a greater effort has
to be made through administrative arrangements and orientation programs to unite the technicians and the multipurpose
workers conceptually and administratively.

India refined the concept of the multipurpose village-
level worker into a practical reality. The obvious merit of
the concept attracted the attention of the organizers of pro-

grams in other countries; and, within a matter of a few years, it was incorporated into the programs of the Philippines and Pakistan.

In each of these countries, central responsibility for the success of the program was placed upon the multipurpose worker. All elements in a community development program were to be tested and fulfilled by the multipurpose worker, and whatever meaning the program was to achieve was to be realized in his day-to-day operation on the village level. He was to be the keystone of the entire program. National support was to provide him with technical support and the commodities required to carry out his program, the political purpose was to constitute his goal, the democratic processes were to be his mode of operation, research and evaluation were to measure the effectiveness of his work, and training was to supply him with the skills he needed to build sound programs. Therefore, the success of the multipurpose village-level worker was to be a major determinant of the success of the total community development program. Needless to say, these goals were never completely realized.

Dual roles are set forth for the multipurpose worker in the documents of AID and its predecessor agencies on community development. These are his role as agent of cultural change and his role as a first-aid extension worker. In performing both roles, the multipurpose worker acts as a liaison between the government and the people of the village. As a first-aid extension agent, he functions as an agriculturalist, an educationist, a health officer, and a recreation leader. When the people of a community want schools, he advises them on how to go about building them; and, when they want to dig more wells, he helps them secure the necessary equipment. The multipurpose worker's functions as a first-aid extension agent closely parallel those of the United States agricultural agent. However, unlike this United States counterpart, the multipurpose worker performs activities in a wide number of technical fields and does not have a highly developed technical competency in any one.

In his role as an agent of change, the multipurpose worker is sometimes identified as a social technician or a cultural innovator. In this capacity, he is not as concerned with the number of roads built or wells dug as he is with what happens to people in the process of achieving material goals.

He is concerned with whether the villagers learn to work together as a community and whether they develop the desire to improve their own lives. His interests go beyond health, economic gains, and educational institutions into the area of attitudes, values, and desires which in the long run, he is taught to believe, are more important than the tangible goals he puts aside for the time being.

At the center of the approach to community development supported by AID and its predecessor agencies is a new type of civil servant, the multipurpose worker, who is trained on the one hand to be a first-aid extension agent for all governmental services at the village level and on the other hand as a catalyzing agent to mobilize the resources of the village people for self-help activities. [8]

What is discussed above represents the ideal version of what the multipurpose worker is and what he does. In practice, an entirely different picture emerges in the actual field situation. In India, the multipurpose worker has been placed under the agricultural extension service. In the Philippines, he is gradually shifting from a multipurpose technical worker to a trainer of locally elected officials. However, the biggest change in the old pattern established in India can be seen in the Comilla project in East Pakistan. Here, specially trained elected village leaders have replaced paid village multipurpose workers. [9]

Ernest Neal believes that, while the multipurpose worker was the answer to field expediency twelve years ago, today trained local government officials can easily assume his task. In mature programs in community development, he states, village people have passed beyond the technical competency of the multipurpose worker. For this reason, he believes that technical services should be upgraded and that the earlier concept of the multipurpose worker should be gradually phased out. [10] Obviously, the debate on the role and the character of the village-level worker has not been resolved. In terms of current patterns, it appears that not one definition but many definitions of the village-level worker will emerge in the next five years. What has worked in Asia certainly is not totally appropriate to Africa, and the answer African community development workers are finding is not totally relevant for Latin America.

TRAINING

A ID and its predecessor agencies have given more attention to training in community development projects than to any other single activity. Foremost among the reasons for this is that the United States had its first large-scale overseas experience with community development in India.

One of the activities India undertook in its first Five-Year Plan was the training of 80, 000 people whose work was related to community development. Social education organizers, village-level workers, block development officers, engineers, overseers, doctors, midwives, women health visitors, and sanitary inspectors were all trained in the concepts and techniques of community development.

India's insistence on the importance of training intensified as its program progressed. In its second Five-Year Plan, development blocks were not open until a full complement of trained staff was available. India never permitted its community development program to outdistance its training capacity. [11] The success of India's program provided the United States with a convincing argument for accepting the premise that training is required if effective community development programs are to be built.

The United States insistence upon the importance of training has played a significant part in professionalizing the field of community development. It has helped attract greater numbers of people to community development work than otherwise would be interested.

Also, it has resulted in the construction of a network of training centers in the aided countries which have introduced ideas that would not have obtained a hearing in the older and more established schools. The concept of democracy, the extension of educational opportunity to the masses, and the principle of mobilizing uneducated villagers in the reconstruction of their own communities are concepts which have found their way into community development training programs even when they are not recognized in the secondary schools and colleges.

RESEARCH AND EVALUATION

Whenever men of learning gather for a long enough

period to discuss a proposed project or an on-going program, there is bound to be talk of research and evaluation. This is equally the case in government offices and in purely academic circles. It is no surprise, therefore, to find that the United States has devoted considerable time, manpower, and financial assistance to the support of research and evaluation activities in the field of community development.

As early as 1955, one year after the Community Development Division of ICA was founded, evaluation teams were sent to India, Pakistan, the Philippines, Egypt, Iran, the Gold Coast, Bolivia, Jamaica, Peru, and Puerto Rico to review the community development programs in each of these countries. Earlier, the United States was directly involved in the creation of the Programme Evaluation Organization of the Government of India, which has become one of the most notable and unusual provisions in India's community development program. The organization has produced numerous reports and studies and has exerted a significant impact on community development policy, programs, and methods. One commentator wrote: "The creation of this organization at the very highest level of the Indian government and staffed by Indian social scientists has put India in the forefront of those countries which are attempting to utilize the social sciences in the planning of national programs."[12]

Administratively, India's Programme Evaluation Organization is associated but outside the Community Development Department. In effect, India has created a small group, separated from any responsibility for decisions and operations of the community development program, with the responsibility for supplying a running account of program operations and for making periodic evaluations of methods and results. This type of relationship enables the Programme Evaluation Organization to publish highly objective and fearlessly critical annual evaluation reports of the workings of the community development program. [13]

In addition, the United States also has played a major role in the creation of a research unit for community development programs in Pakistan. The organizational structure of the Pakistani research program is much different than India's. In Pakistan, the research group operates within the Community Development Department. Those who argue for this type of approach claim that the existence of the research

group within a community development department enables
the researchers to obtain a more realistic picture of the
actual operations of the department and also provides them
with a greater opportunity to implement their research findings. Those who question this approach claim that, under this
arrangement, h o n e s t y and objectivity are much harder to
achieve.

The third country in which the United States has exerted
significant influence upon research and evaluation activities
is the Philippines.   Here, there is yet another organizational
structure for the research program. Like India, the research
group is outside the Community Development Department.
However, unlike India, it is not located within another arm of
the government, but outside the government in a university.

This format was established largely through the efforts
of Ernest E. Neal and Harry Naylor, both of whom were
social scientists and specialists in community development
with ICA in the Philippines. Through their efforts, the Presidential Assistant for Community Development and the
University of the Philippines agreed to organize a community
development research center at the university. The center
is staffed with social scientists from the various disciplines
in the university and has as its major objective the evaluation
of the Philippine community development program through
research studies in the basic concepts. The purpose of the
Community Development Research Council is:

> . . . to set up a cooperative endeavor between the
> University and Presidential Assistant for a quali-
> tative evaluation of the methodology employed in
> the Philippine Community Development Program
> in order to determine better ways and means to
> increase the effectiveness of the Program; and to
> create a research organization under the auspices
> of the University. [14]

Much of the research in the United States in matters
related to the field of community development is carried on
in university research centers. Therefore, the Philippine
research program in community development is familiar to
American social scientists. Many argue that it is the best
possible arrangement in that it brings to the field of community development social scientists and university facilities
which otherwise would not be available. The success of the
research program in the Philippines affirms the soundness

of these arguments.

In India, Pakistan, and the Philippines, the United States provided strong initial stimulation and continuing support for research and evaluation programs. The difference in the administrative framework of the research programs in each of these countries provides an excellent example of the flexibility of the United States in meeting the needs of different cultures. However, the more important point is not the flexibility but the fact that the United States played a vital role in creating research and evaluation programs in the field of community development.

THE SELF-HELP PRINCIPLE

Technical assistance is not a one-sided activity but is a cooperative venture. The purpose goes beyond the mere performance of a technical function by a technician and includes an attempt to bring about a decided change in the recipient. Those who acquire technical knowledge and skills are expected to come away from the exchange with the inspiration and the determination to work on their own. Then, and only then, is technical assistance adjudged successful.

The type of change called for in this definition of technical assistance is slow in occurring and difficult to bring about. Often United States aid programs accomplish the reverse of what they set out to achieve. Many of the recipient nations become overly dependent upon the United States. This, of course, is the antithesis of the primary objective of a self-help program. Some nations become so accustomed to receiving help from the United States that they lose the urge to continue the task of development alone. When this happens, the technical cooperation program is a failure.

The habit of self-help is a prerequisite for survival in the modern world. Those who need help greatly outnumber those who can or who are disposed to give it. Many live out their entire lives without receiving the most elementary forms of aid simply because there are not enough people who will help them.

Theoretically, United States technical assistance activities are planned to meet these problems by reducing the need for large amounts of outside help by increasing the impact of the small amounts that are provided. This principle is so closely identified with the United States' interpretation of technical assistance that one ICA publication on technical cooperation is entitled The Dramatic Story of Helping Others to Help Themselves. [15]

This interpretation of technical assistance shifts the emphasis from what the United States does to what the receiving country does. Technical cooperation is looked upon as a joint activity in which enterprises begin with United States aid, but do not end with it. American technical aid is used as a booster and a stimulant and is never planned to be so adequate that it completes the job at hand. The contribution made by the receiving country has to be greater in the long run than that made by the United States.

The aid programs in Latin America provide an example, on the financial level, of the cooperative aspects of United States technical assistance activities. In 1958, for instance, the United States provided $38 million in aid and the individual countries spent $52.4 million on joint enterprises. [16] The joint financing of a project is used by the United States as a tangible measure of the seriousness of the aided country's intention to help itself.

The principle of self-help is especially appropriate to the concept of community development supported by AID and its predecessor agencies. In the area of community development, AID stresses the importance of changing the way people look at their responsibilities and of giving assistance that supplements but never replaces initiative or local effort.

The self-help principle is closely related to the development of democratic values and processes which is an important concept in the United States' definition of community development. One of the major aspects of the concept of democracy is the principle of "by the people." This, of course, is another way of saying self-help.

THE POLITICAL PURPOSE

Great efforts are made to broadcast the fact that vast numbers of the world's population are hungry, diseased, and impoverished. However, the fact that, in addition, many of these same people are voiceless is often neglected. Basically, community development, which is aimed at giving local people a voice in their government, serves as a correction to this problem.

Although community development personnel in AID recognize the importance of economic goals, the traditionally powerful emphasis upon economic goals forces them to give primary emphasis to political objectives. Harry Naylor summarizes the community development position on this question in a special report distributed in 1959. He said: "Technical assistance . . . in developing more representative government is . . . of equal importance with . . . technical assistance to the economic sectors."[17]

Recent activities in Laos provide a dramatic example that once men are schooled in the skills of self-government they do not lose them easily. Despite the collapse of the central government and subsequent disorder, the only United States aid program to continue functioning in Laos was the community development program, which worked through and strengthened units of local government.[18] This was reassuring to those who look upon community development as a valuable instrument in building systems of local government.

It is more than a coincidence that the most successful programs in community development overseas supported by United States funds are those in developing nations whose national leaders understand and trust democratic ideals.[19] Arthur Dunham states that community development is basically democratic in philosophy. He feels that, logically, it is tied up with such ideas as ultimate control by the people, a substantial degree of freedom by individuals and groups, a considerable amount of government decentralization, and widespread citizen participation. Thus, a national community development program reaches its highest degree of effectiveness only in a country where democracy prevails. It is reasonable to expect, therefore, that the closer a country is to totalitarian or feudal patterns the less likely the emergency of community development will be in that country.[20]

Jack D. Mezirow, AID staff member, defines the primary purpose of community development as that of helping people who make up a community to function productively as democratic members of problem-solving groups.[21] This definition implies that faith in people and in the democratic way of life are prerequisites for effective programs.

Within the framework of this view, community development is used as a device for helping governments reach out to their people to help them become more active participants in the life of their nations. Local initiative is offered as a cardinal virtue; and people on the local level are encouraged to organize themselves for planning and action, to define their common and individual needs and problems, and to make group and individual plans to meet their needs and solve their problems. Governments committed to this concept are expected to help their people to learn techniques for cooperative action and to organize self-help programs. [22]

It is only when the role of the democratic processes and values in community development are fully understood that it becomes clear that the community development personnel of AID are not primarily interested in increased agricultural production, better roads, or better health conditions. They are more interested in process than in material products. It is not so much the actual problems as the way people deal with the problems and the way people learn from these problems that is of primary concern to the community development staff.

This outlook is confirmed in a report written by Boyd Faulkner while on assignment in Tanzania for AID. He notes that an important influence AID advisers have had upon the community development program to Tanzania has been the securing of common agreement among community development officials that there must be incorporated into the program the means of assuring the ordinary citizen opportunity to share in making important decisions about his living conditions and the guarantees that plans and demands will not be imposed from above. [23]

Among the most impressive proofs that political goals can be achieved through a community development program are to be found in the Philippines, where an association of barrio councils which strengthened the concept of self-government among local peoples was formed in 1960; fifty-four provincial and 437 municipal community development councils were activated, and a law establishing rural local autonomy was passed. All of these activities were encouraged by

United States technical assistance specialists in the field of community development through the office of the Presidential Assistant for Community Development on the assumption that political change is the forerunner of economic growth. The sharp increase in economic productivity that followed the strengthening of the nation's community development program substantiated the soundness of the assumption.

The Philippine program proves that economic development is strongly influenced by noneconomic factors. Attitudes, values, motivation, and political considerations loom quite as large as the available supply of capital in determining the course of economic growth. Robert B. Morrow of the ICA staff, speaking from his experience in the Philippines, reports that the Philippine community development program made a substantial contribution to economic development even though economic factors were not always paramount in the choice of projects. In this regard, he said that a functional local government and a feeling of confidence between the village people and the government agencies are prime requisites for sustained economic growth. [24]

The recognition of the importance of the political objective is not completely original to AID and its predecessor agencies. As early as 1943, the Advisory Committee on Education in the Colonies of the British Colonial Office wrote that "the development of political institutions and political power until the day arrives when the people can become self-governing" is one of the foremost goals of mass education. [25] And again, in 1958, representatives from seventeen British territories and former territories where there had been community development programs concluded that:

> Community development is not a method of doing economic development on the cheap and success cannot be measured by adding up the material projects completed. They are but means to a social and political end. The product of successful community development is not wells, roads, schools, and new crops. It is stable, self-reliant communities with an assured sense of social and political responsibility. [26]

In addition, community development has proven to be an effective weapon against Communism in the Cold War. Its emphasis upon giving the people of newly emergent nations a stronger stake in the political life of their nations tended to correct the conditions which bred Communism. Time magazine reported that community development had been the Philippines' most effective weapon against the Communist-led guerillas. [27] This kind of success in the Philippines and elsewhere places community development at the center of the struggle between democracy and Communism.

In emphasizing the political objective, community development specialists find that they have a fine talking point for explaining the distinction between community development and other programs seeking change on the village level. Community development workers often are accused of duplicating the work of the health, agriculture, and education departments. In emphasizing the political objective, they have a claim to activities which are clearly unique.

Unfortunately, the United States has not been able to implement the political goal in all of the countries it has aided. Part of the difficulty is the intangibility of social and political activities. Also, the developing nations have a compulsion to stress those things which produce immediate and visible results. This, of course, is easily understood. Hungry people are more interested in talking about bread than about democracy, and diseased people are more concerned about curing their own ailments than they are in curing the social ills of the community. For this reason, many thoughtful observers sincerely wonder if it is realistic to place so much emphasis upon democracy in nations where people still have not achieved an adequate standard of living. Undaunted, United States community development personnel overseas stand firmly by their convictions that material goods can be achieved within the framework of democracy and freedom and, therefore, they must assist the needy peoples of the world to advance politically as well as economically.

NOTES TO CHAPTER 2

[1] United States Technical Cooperation Administration, Community Services Staff, "Methods of Obtaining Participation in Self-help Activities" (Washington, D. C.: U. S. Technical Cooperation Administration, 1953), p. 9.

[2]Louis Miniclier, "Report of the SEATO Conference on Community Development, Baguio City, Philippines, December 7-16, 1961." Copy found in the country files under "Philippines 1961," Community Development Division, ICA, Washington, D.C.

[3]Carl C. Taylor,"Making a Community Development Program Work," Practical Considerations: How to Build a Community Development Program, Background Paper V for the 1961 Inter-Regional Community Development Conference (Washington, D.C.: Community Development Division, ICA, 1961), p. 10.

[4]United Nations, Bureau of Social Affairs, International Survey of Programs of Social Development (New York: United Nations, 1959), p. 156.

[5]Lucian W. Pye, "The Social and Political Implications of Community Development," Political Implications of Community Development, Background Paper IV for the 1961 Inter-Regional Community Development Conference (Washington, D.C.: Community Development Division, ICA, 1961), p. 39.

[6]United Nations, Administrative Committee on Coordination to Economic and Social Council, "Twentieth Report," Document E/2931, October 18, 1956, Annex III. Reprinted by Community Development Division, ICA, n.d., pp. 5-6.

[7]Irwin T. Sanders, Community Development and National Change (Washington, D.C.: Community Development Division, ICA, 1958), p. 56.

[8]Harry L. Naylor, "Urged Culture Change in the Philippine Community Development Program, "Practical Considerations: How to Build a Community Development Program, Background Paper V for the 1961 Inter-Regional Community Development Conference, op. cit., p. 28.

[9]Ernest Neal, A Report to the Assistant Administrator for Technical Cooperation and Research on the Agency for International Development Program of Community Development Assistance (Washington, D.C.: AID, 1964), pp. 12-13.

[10]Ibid., pp. 4-6.

[11]U. L. Goswami, "Three Facets of Community Development," Community Development Bulletin, I (January, 1956), 12-15.

[12]Howard H. Beers, "Evaluation in Community Development--The Indian Experience," Community Development: Evaluation, Background Paper VI for the 1961 Inter-Regional Community Development Conference (Washington, D. C.: Community Development Division, ICA, 1961), p. 14.

[13]Ibid., pp. 14-15.

[14]Buenaventura M. Villaneuva, A Study of the Competence of Barrio Citizens to Conduct Barrio Government (Quezon City, Philippines: Community Development Research Council, The University of the Philippines, 1959), p. v.

[15]United States ICA, The Dramatic Story of Helping Others to Help Themselves, Department of State Publication 6815 (Washington, D. C.: Government Printing Office, 1959), p. 58.

[16]Ibid., p. 23.

[17]Harry L. Naylor, "Special Report: The Community Development Program Is Based on Local Government" (Manila: ICA, 1959), pp. i-ii.

[18]United States ICA, Community Development Division, "Community Development Conference, Seoul, Korea, May 6-12, 1961, Briefing and Background for Senior Representative of the United States" (Washington, D. C.: The Division, 1961), unnumbered.

[19]Carl C. Taylor, op. cit., p. 22.

[20]Arthur Dunham, "Community Development--Its Nature and Characteristics, A Working Memorandum." Copy found on file in United States AID, Washington, D. C.

[21]Jack D. Mezirow, "Community Development Extension and Village Aid Synthesis," Community Development Information, II (January-February, 1961), 6-8.

[22]United States ICA, Community Development Division, "The Community Development Guidelines of the International Cooperation Administration" (Washington, D. C.: The Division, 1956), pp. 1-2.

[23]Boyd Faulkner, "Project History and Analysis Report on Community Development in the United Republic of Tanzania for the Period of January 1, 1962, to December 31, 1964" (Washington, D. C.: AID, 1965), p. 10.

[24]Robert B. Morrow, "The Project Concept in Community Development" (Manila: United States Operations Mission, ICA, n. d.), p. 4.

[25]United Kingdom, Advisory Committee on Education in the Colonies, Mass Education in African Society (London: Her Majesty's Stationery Office, 1943), p. 4.

[26]United Kingdom, Colonial Office, Community Development--A Handbook (London: Her Majesty's Stationery Office, 1958), p. 65.

[27]"The Philippines, Road to the Twentieth Century," Time, LXXVII (December 12, 1960), 31.

CHAPTER **3** FUNCTIONS PERFORMED
BY COMMUNITY DEVEL-
OPMENT PERSONNEL
IN THE UNITED STATES
TECHNICAL ASSISTANCE
PROGRAMS

The major functions fall into four general categories, all
of which have educational components. They are: (1) advisory
assistance, (2) training, (3) material assistance and dollar
aid, and (4) informational services.

These functions are not performed directly on the village level, but rather are supportive over-all developmental
services. The village constitutes only one level of a total
community development program in any given country. Behind every village-level program there is a large team of
technical and administrative personnel operating within the
framework of the governmental structure.

United States community development personnel overseas, for the most part, work with people who are one or
more steps removed from the village people themselves.
Ordinarily, United States staffs do not engage in such grass-
root-level activities as agricultural extension, literacy
training, or the organization of cooperatives.

Instead, they train the teachers of village-level workers, engage in research and experimentation related to specific problems faced by the village workers, and help organize and sometimes administer the technical departments
required to support community development programs. [1]

Many of the AID staff function at the highest level of
governmental operations, usually in an advisory capacity,
with government officials of cabinet or ministerial rank. For
this reason, the phrase "shirtsleeve diplomacy," frequently
used to describe the work of United States technicians in
developing nations, does not accurately describe the kind of
work most community development advisers find themselves
doing. A better phrase would be "coatsleeve diplomacy."
A technician not only needs technical skills, but also has to
be somewhat of a linguist, a diplomat, a teacher, a sociologist, a cultural anthropologist, and a missionary. [2]

Many of these functions also are performed by personnel working for the United Nations and its specialized agencies. The United Nations implements its objectives through the dissemination of reports, studies, and publications and the organization of seminars and conferences. It also grants fellowships for visits and study abroad and establishes pilot projects and training centers. In addition, it dispatches experts around the world to help the developing nations plan programs and train indigenous staffs. [3]

ADVISORY ASSISTANCE

One of AID's basic documents on community development lists the primary role of its specialists as that of advising governments on the organization and administration of community development programs. [4] In this document, advisory assistance is placed at the forefront of all of the functions performed by members of the staff. Within the framework of this directive, technical assistance goes beyond the mere performance of a technical skill by a foreign expert and becomes, more properly, the transmission of knowledge, skills, and attitudes.

Leonard J. Saccio, one-time Deputy Director of the ICA, supported this point of view in an address he gave at a conference in 1958:

> . . . we would be providing for only half the job
> if we provided only for the construction of a road
> by an American contractor. The road would be
> built, true. But what would we have accomplished
> if the people of that country are not able to maintain it? . . . So our American contractor and our
> Bureau of Public Roads must undertake the job of
> education and the development of governmental
> institutions as well as that of physical construction of a highway. The same is true of almost any
> other activity undertaken in the mutual security
> program. [5]

This interpretation of technical cooperation by both the United States and cooperating governments means that advice is sought and given on such matters as organization, training, and the philosophy best suited for establishing a sound community development program.

At various times in the history of United States involvement in community development programs overseas, this has meant that anthropologists, social workers, sociologists, and specialists in the area of arts and crafts have had to be recruited and sent to the countries requesting particular help in these areas.

The advisers sent to cooperating countries work with partners from the host countries who usually have some competence in the same technical field as theirs. This enables the technician to affect a direct exchange of knowledge on a day-to-day basis. The local technician assigned to work with the foreign technician is called a counterpart. Frequently, the counterpart is a key person within his own country.

This arrangement serves two purposes. First, it enables the United States adviser to train someone to carry on his job after he leaves the country. Second, by working with a key official in the host country, the adviser has close access to an important channel of influence which in time broadens the impact of his assistance efforts.

The principle underlying the placement of a technician on a level where the greatest number of people can be affected by his work is called the "multiplier principle." It is such a vital part of the over-all philosophy of the United States that, at one time, the agency published a quarterly entitled The Multiplier.

Advisory assistance is the most important function performed by United States community development personnel overseas. Since this is the case, there is very little question that the primary item in any technical cooperation program is the adviser sent to transmit skill and knowledge.

THE EXCHANGE OF INFORMATION

The exchange of information in the form of the written word in books, reports, digests, pamphlets, magazines, the replies to special inquiries, and the entire range of visual media in films, filmstrips, slides, cartoons, graphics, and exhibits, and the spoken word in conferences, seminars, lectures, and casual conversations is a second important function performed by AID.

Information is exchanged within two systems, the internal and the external. The internal informational system serves the staff of AID, whereas, the external informational system is directed to those outside AID, particularly to those in cooperating countries, who look to AID for assistance.

The development of guidance material on community development and the exchange of information and experience gained as a result of bilateral and multilateral governmental and non-governmental experience are listed as one of the functions of United States community development staff in "The Community Development Guidelines."

In fulfilling this function over the years, the United States community development staff, along with the staff working for the United Nations, has become an important source of reports, studies, and publications on community development. Among the publications issued are the reports of three teams of United States consultants to the ICA and its predecessor agency, the Foreign Operations Administration, who observed community development programs in developing countries; a bibliography on community development; and the highly regarded Community Development Review. Starting with the first issue in 1956, the Review was published on a quarterly basis until 1964.

Among the major conferences and seminars organized and supported by the United States were the Conference on Community Development at the Center for International Studies at the Massachusetts Institute of Technology in 1957; the Southeast Asia Treaty Organization Conference on Community Development in Baguio City, Philippines, in 1960; and the Inter-Regional Community Development Conference in Seoul, Korea, in 1961. Other conferences have been held in Iran in 1955, in Thailand in 1956, in Libya in 1958, and in Ceylon in 1959. These conferences served to enhance the effectiveness of community development programs in the host countries and improved the professional competency of the United States community development advisers attending the conferences.

All of these activities describe the information services provided on an international level. Nationally, each community development staff member located in a cooperating country is AID's local information center for those who require his assistance.

The other informational system is the internal informational service which AID provides for its own employees. The purpose of this system is to keep the staff abreast of the latest developments in the field and of policy changes within the agency and to assist them in maintaining their competence as specialists. This informational system is built upon the experience of staff members in the field and upon the findings of scholars studying community development and related subjects. The program, for the most part, consists of the provision of materials for technicians before they go overseas and of the distribution of reports, memoranda, evaluation studies, and official publications to those on the staff. In sum, the internal informational system refers to the exchange of materials among the staff within the agency.

Community development necessitates a highly trained and informed staff at all levels. If competence is required of locals in the host country at all levels, then it goes without question that it is an important requirement for advisers. Thus, the existence of a good internal informational system is of prime importance for a successful technical assistance program in the field of community development.

FORMAL TRAINING

AID is involved in formal training activities in two ways. First, training is provided for participants in the United States and third countries; and, secondly, training programs for local people are strongly supported in all the countries where AID sponsors community development activities.

Through participant training, AID is able to give selected leaders from cooperating countries an opportunity to learn the principles of community development and to observe actual programs which utilize these principles in the United States and third countries. This method of training is particularly valuable for explaining a concept such as democracy to people who live in countries where democracy has never been a viable part of the nation's history. The opportunity to visit a democratic country and to live in a democratic system teaches the participants much more than they could ever learn from books. This is one of the reasons why participant training has become an important part of

United States technical assistance programs.

Training programs for local community development workers and those in allied fields are strongly encouraged in all countries where the United States supports community development programs. In India, Pakistan, the Philippines, and Tanzania, just to mention a few nations, a considerable amount of time has been devoted to building, staffing, and supporting training programs. The strong support of community development training programs for local personnel is looked upon as an important means of implementing the United States philosophy of community development in assisted nations.

MATERIAL ASSISTANCE AND DOLLAR AID

In many places a machine, large or small, simple or complex, is all that is needed to solve a problem that has existed for centuries. For this reason, demonstration supplies and equipment are supplied in limited amounts to cooperating countries under the terms of the United States technical cooperation programs. In India, for instance, transport equipment and teaching aids were provided; and, in other countries, demonstration and laboratory equipment for health programs and heavy highway equipment for training mechanics and operators are supplied.

United States material support and dollar aid in the field of community development is not limited to the aid permitted under the terms of the technical cooperation program. In 1960, for instance, the United States paid for over 50 per cent of the cost of the community development program in the Philippines and 58 per cent of the Korean program. Obviously, funds were taken from sources other than those normally provided for under the technical cooperation title. Actually, aid was given to these countries out of funds set aside for defense support, special assistance, and Public Law 480 local currency counterpart funds. [6]

Counterpart funds are local currency funds deposited by the local government in a special account in the country's own name and available for its use to carry out the objectives of the United States foreign aid program. Under the terms of the law governing these funds, foreign governments have to deposit to the counterpart account an amount equal to the proceeds accruing to them from the import and sale of special United States commodities.

Funds from sources other than the technical cooperation title were used in the Philippines for project costs such as salaries of training, information, and office staff; t r a i n i n g costs of new r e c r u i t s and their salaries for at least six months to a year; support costs of institutes for lay leaders; in-service training for technicians of supporting agencies; research and evaluation studies; and grants-in-aid.

In India, funds g i v e n for the community development programs were used for jeeps, station wagons, health vans, motor graders, tractors, road rollers, t r a i l e r s and film projectors, d r i l l i n g rigs, printing equipment, X-ray sets, a d d r e s s sets, record players, refrigerators, insemination sets, centrifuges, and other farm tools. The v a r i e t y of items g i v e n to these countries indicates the far-reaching scope of material assistance and dollar aid in United States programs.

The major questions on material aid no longer deal with whether such aid is a good thing. Material aid has proved its value and United States programs are so deeply committed to its use that such questions are purely academic.

However, an important question remains; and that deals with the efficient utilization of material support and dollar aid. Large amounts of money and big shipments of machines are new phenomena in many of the nations receiving them, and these nations generally cannot use such aid properly unless someone shows them how. This calls for intensive training programs, the cost of which is only a fraction of the money wasted where training does not accompany the introduction of dollar aid and machinery in large quantities.

NOTES TO CHAPTER 3

[1]United Nations, Administrative Committee on Coordination to the Economic and Social Council, "Twentieth Report," Document E/2931, October 18, 1956, Annex III. Reprinted by Community Development Division, ICA, n. d. , p. 11.

[2] United States Congress, Technical Assistance, Report No. 139, 85th Congress, 1st Session (Washington, D. C.: Government Printing Office, 1957), pp. 42–43.

[3] United Nations, Bureau of Social Affairs, Social Progress Through Community Development (New York: United Nations, 1955), p. 14.

[4] United States ICA, Community Development Division, "The Community Development Guidelines of the International Cooperation Administration" (Washington, D. C.: The Division, 1956), p. 3.

[5] Leonard J. Saccio, The Educational Challenge in Underdeveloped Areas, Department of State Publication 6793 (Washington, D. C.: Government Printing Office, 1959) p. 5.

[6] United Nations, Bureau of Social Affairs, International Survey of Programs of Social Development (New York: United Nations, 1959), p. 165.

4

COMMUNITY DEVELOPMENT AS AN EDUCATIONAL PROCESS

SCHOOLING AND EDUCATION

In most developing countries, there are vast areas where schools do not exist, or if they do exist, they are totally inadequate. The important question in these areas is not how to relate the school to community development, but rather how the educational process can be set in motion without the benefit of a school. A distinction between the meaning of education and schooling has to be made before the problem this latter question presents can be solved.

Most people are so accustomed to identifying education with schooling that they have lost sight of the fact that, fundamentally, education is a process and that schools are the accidental and expendable institutions where the processes take place. The distinction is simple and clear-cut.

The term "education," as used by AID personnel in overseas projects, refers to the processes involved in the transfer of skills, knowledge, and attitudes. These processes are as much a part of the formal educational program of a training college as they are of an informal agricultural redevelopment scheme or a cultural mission. This is the broad definition of education.

When knowledge, skills, and attitudes are deliberately transmitted, the processes of education are activated whether the transmission takes place in a Western-style classroom, a village marketplace, the bush, the wheat field, or a hut. In most of the underdeveloped countries where technical cooperation programs operate, the everyday world of the villager of necessity becomes a classroom. It is in this out-of-the-way, roundabout, informal classroom where villagers first learn that they can develop, that they must develop, and that they will eventually learn how to develop.

A village-level worker who shows the wife of a subsistent farmer how to preserve fruit is an educator; a local technician who demonstrates an improved technique of plowing to a group of farmers is an educator; and a villager, only newly literate himself, who teaches his fellow villagers how to read is also an educator. One United States technical assistance administrator is so convinced of this that he maintains that technical cooperation programs have no need for a separate educational branch because basically every technician is an educator. [1]

Therefore, when a village-level worker and a villager face one another and interact in such a way that the villager is able to walk away knowing more than he did when he approached the situation, the processes of education are at work. It is this elemental idea which is at the basis of the concept that community development is an educational process. The full understanding of the meaning of education in its broadest definition and as a process is fundamental to the full acceptance of the idea that community development is an educational process.

COMMUNITY DEVELOPMENT AS A PROCESS

Irwin T. Sanders says that most people emphasize one or the other of the four aspects of community development in their discussions. Those who stress goals and objectives are mostly concerned with method; those who emphasize activity are concerned with programs; those who promote the idea of community development as it is interpreted by its devotees are concerned with it as a movement; and those who place emphasis upon what happens to people are concerned with process. [2]

AID community development staffs are largely concerned with community development as a process. In the first paragraph of the "Guidelines," community development is described as a "process of social action in which the people . . . organize and define . . . needs and problems . . . make group and individual plans . . . and supplement (their own) resources when necessary."[3] The emphasis throughout the document is upon what happens to village people when they participate in community-betterment projects.

In a joint article, two United States community devel-

opment staff members write that a good community development program seeks to achieve its goals through an educational process in which the attitudes, the concepts, and the
goals of the village people are changed. The authors describe program goals in terms of the changes that occur in
the villagers who participate in village projects. A successful program, they feel, changes village people from passive,
nonparticipating members of the community to citizens
capable of democratic participation in community problem
solving. [4]

Dr. Harry Naylor, another staff member, interprets
the purposes of community development in much the same
way. He describes a satisfactory program as one in which
the processes of village activity are directed to changing attitudes among the village people. [5] Ernest Neal, an AID staff
member in the Philippines, describes community development
as a process through which villagers develop the aspiration
and the determination to undertake community development
projects. [6]

THE EDUCATIONAL PROCESS

The distinction between a school and a church cannot be
given by describing the kind of bricks or mortar used in the
building because the meanings of these buildings are not contained in their material composition. The real meaning of
these buildings exists in the minds of the men who use them.
The same is true of the outlook on community development
held by those responsible for these programs within AID and
its predecessor agencies. By and large, the staff does not
measure program success in terms of the number of material
objects added to a community, but rather in terms of changed
attitudes, skills, and knowledge among the people.

This emphasis upon the development of people first,
foremost, and always is not seen as detrimental to the economic growth of the nations aided. Development economists
have long recognized the correlation between the quality of
people and economic development. James Green, a community development adviser for AID, states in support of this
view: ". . . the personal habits and traits associated with
the use of capital -- among them initiative, prudence, inge-
nuity, and foresightedness -- gave a deeper and surer base to a
nation's economic advance than the blueprints of a planning
commission. "[7]

Change, economic or otherwise, occurs through living individuals; and it is upon these human beings that the forces for change have to be brought to bear. The community development staff within AID uses this principle to substantiate their view that community development is a person-centered process. Schools, roads, and the increase of crop yields are still considered important, but only insofar as they provide tangible evidence of the development of persons.

The primary change sought is a change in people. The achievement of this goal rests upon the awakening of needs, the removal of resistances to the means required to satisfy needs, and the improvement of the technical skills necessary to achieve felt needs. The realization of all of these goals involves basic changes in attitudes, skills, and knowledge.

The alteration or acquisition of new attitudes, knowledge, and skills is another way of expressing the primary objective of the United States concept of community development. Since a change in attitudes, knowledges, and skills is basically an educational process, community development is an educational process. Community development is initiated through discussions and the analysis of local problems. It embodies all the arts of persuasion, extending knowledge, and learning new skills. Essentially, the process is the same whether it is conducted in a formal or an informal setting or whether it is applied to literacy, health, agriculture, or road building.

Jack Mezirow, speaking from his experience as a community development adviser, states that community development is an educational process and that the work of the community development practitioner is educational. Community development workers, he states, need special competence in teaching democratic human relations, group discussions, action methods, and the application of the scientific method to the solution of common problems. [8]

Coolie Verner's distinction between community development and community action provides a solid foundation for claiming that community development is an educational process. Mr. Verner defines community development as an educational process in which people learn how to be responsible citizens by participating in the solution of common problems. Community development, he maintains, is the process which leads to community action, but is not to be confused with community action. He clarifies the distinction between community development and c o m m u n i t y action by pointing out that community action can and does occur without the specific education that strengthens democracy while, on the other hand, community development or e d u c a t i o n for action cannot occur without producing cooperative community action.

Mr. Verner maintains that the educational process is more important than the tangible results achieved. He believes the important thing is not the construction of a community center but whether the individuals who build the center become more i n t e l l i g e n t and more active in community activities. [9]

This distinction between the educational and the activity phases of community development should in no way suggest that community action is unimportant. Along with other criteria, community action provides a means of measuring the success of a community development program. Also, dramatic physical accomplishments serve to m o t i v a t e village people to continue in the work of community betterment.

IMPLICATIONS

There are at least four implications, from an educational point of view, of the concept of community development expressed in this chapter. Only some of t h e s e have been recognized by AID and its p r e d e c e s s o r agencies. First, c o m m u n i t y development workers have to be thought of as educators and the villagers as learners. Second, community development workers have to be trained in educational techniques. Third, community development has to be integrated i n t o the total educational system of a country; and fourth, community development programs have to be distinguished in content and in purpose from those undertaken by the technical departments of a national government.

Similar to educators all over the world, the village-level worker should understand his learners -- in this case, the village people. This knowledge should be based upon extensive research in the customs, habits, aspirations, attitudes, interests, temperaments, and abilities of the individuals or groups with whom he works. In addition, he should utilize

learning devices in his work with villagers. These devices
can be as simple as the use of local wood in a demonstration
lesson or as complex as a scientific experiment. Also, educational concepts -- such as readiness, individual differences,
self-development, and motivation -- should play a determining
role in the thinking of all community development workers.

The definition of community development reflected in
the writings of the United States community development staff
calls for a new kind of government employee who is an educator rather than a manipulative or a managerial bureaucrat.
In the past, governmental, professional leadership planned for
the community rather than with it. Programs often were conducted under the name of community development when, in
fact, they were no more than institutional activities used as
vehicles to achieve a technical department's specific goals.
The normal leadership pattern, therefore, was not educative.

Grace Langley, a United States community development
adviser, composed a list of what she thought the duties of
village-level workers were while she was in India. The list
included such items as the teaching of improved techniques of
farming, the organization of campaigns for introducing extension and cash crops, and the demonstration of the uses of
improved seed and fertilizers. [10] Each of these duties has a
significant educational component which clearly justifies call-
ing the village-level workers who use them "educators" and the
villagers they work with "learners. "

Since the village-level workers are educators, it is
extremely important that they be trained to use education's
vast body of theory and practice, particularly in such areas
as learning theory, audio-visual aids, and group dynamics.
Training in the use of audio-visual materials is particularly
important. Most village audiences are illiterate,and, thus,
need materials to picture what they cannot read. Audio-
visual materials are also required to bring village people out
to learn and to maintain their attention while they are there.
In the process of stimulating community awareness, the use
of posters, books, and pamphlets are also useful and should
receive special attention in training programs.

Another implication is the need to integrate community
development programs into the total education program of a
country. The coordination of educational activities on every

level and under every guise makes sense both from a financial and an educational point of view. Logically, community
development should be coordinated with formal education.
Unfortunately, this has not been achieved to any great degree
in the countries where the United States has supported programs.

The university can provide research and evaluation
services, special seminars for senior community development personnel, and training facilities for multipurpose village-level workers. The secondary school can provide preservice training for students who expect to go into the field
of community development and citizenship courses for all
students. The primary schools, by relating their curricula
to community needs and resources, can help their students to
learn the importance of assuming active participation in the
lives of their communities. In addition, from time to time
the primary school can provide programs which will be of
interest and of value to both the adults and the young people of
the community. These examples demonstrate the close relationship that can exist between community development and
formal education.

Community development programs should also be coordinated with informal educational activities. The family,
religious groups, other government programs, and commercial enterprises are all engaged in the business of education
in one form or another and provide points of integration and
coordination with ongoing community development programs.

Finally, in emphasizing the role of education in community development, a strong case must be made for maintaining that community development is different in content and
purpose than programs undertaken by technical departments.
Community development is more than the sum total of social
work, adult education, agricultural education, and the other
fields which serve as its sources. As Louis Miniclier says,
"Community development borrowed freely but has its own
identity. "[11]

CONCLUSION

It is most important to look at community development
as a process which is people-centered, democratic in philosophy, and educational in character. Although slower and un-

certain at times, a definition of community development which assigns a central place to education results in a program which helps people to want to develop their own communities and at the same time achieves results which are lasting.

Those who look at community development in these terms define community development as an effort to bring about human change. Education, they feel, is involved not only when a community development program operates through a school or when a literacy campaign is organized or when a fundamental education program is established, but, in addition, is an important ingredient in every community development activity.

NOTES TO CHAPTER 4

[1] Jonathan B. Bingham, Shirt-sleeve Diplomacy (New York: J. Day Company, 1954), p. 21.

[2] Irwin T. Sanders, "Theories of Community Development, " Rural Sociology, XXIII (March, 1958), 2.

[3] United States ICA, Community Development Division, "The Community Development Guidelines of the International Cooperation Administration"(Washington, D. C. :The Division,1956), p. 1.

[4] Jack D. Mezirow and Frank A. Santopolo, "Five Years of Community Development in Pakistan, " Village Aid (Lahore, West Pakistan: Village-AID Administration, 1960), pp. 115-16.

[5] Harry L. Naylor, "Community Development and Traditional Behavior Patterns" (Washington, D. C. : Community Development Division, ICA, 1960), p. 5.

[6] Ernest Neal, "The Community Development Approach to Economic Development and Democratic Government in Underdeveloped Countries" (Manila: ICA, 1957), p. 9.

[7] James W. Green, "Community Development as Economic Development: The Role of Value Orientations, " Community Development Review, V (September, 1960), 12-13.

[8]Jack D. Mezirow, "Community Development, Extension of the Village Aid Synthesis, " Community Development Information, II (January–February, 1961), 8.

[9]Coolie Verner, "The Community Development Process, " lecture delivered at the Community Leadership Workshop, University of Wisconsin, Madison, Wisc., October 27, 1959, pp. 3–4. Copy found in the files of the Community Development Division, ICA, Washington, D.C.

[10]Grace E. Langley, "Community Development Programs, Republic of India" (Washington, D.C.: Community Development Division, ICA, n.d.), p. 18.

[11]Louis Miniclier, "Social Group Work in Community Development Programs," Community Organization 1960 (New York: Columbia University Press, 1960), p. 117.

CHAPTER **5** THE EDUCATIONAL
ASPECTS OF
ADVISORY ASSISTANCE

A DEFINITION OF ADVISORY ASSISTANCE[1]

The term advisory assistance has come to mean to AID
a voluntary association in which the staff of the agency enters
into temporary relationships with representatives from other
countries in order to help them solve their existing problems
through professional assistance.

AID feels that the workability of the agreements it
enters depends upon an awareness among those in the cooperating countries that the goals of the joint program will not be
realized unless the program is built upon mutual support and
close cooperation. The agency, bound up as it is in the
democratic tradition and committed to the principle of helping
people through their own efforts to help themselves, places
great emphasis upon the need for purely voluntary agreements which are free of all pressures. The agency believes
that anything less than a completely free and voluntary association borders on imperialism.

This emphasis upon the formation of voluntary associations is based upon sound motivational theory. Educators
and social workers have long recognized that helping activities are likely to succeed only if there is a willingness on the
part of the receiver to accept the help. This is equally true
whether advice is exchanged among individuals or among
nations.

Another element in the agency's definition of advisory
assistance is professionalism. President Truman, in his
inaugural address, said that the material resources the
United States can provide the needy peoples of the world are
sorely limited, but that it has immeasurable resources of
technical knowledge which are almost inexhaustible.[2]

The amount of assistance needed by developing countries is greater than the United States or any other nation

can supply. United States technical assistance programs were established to channel whatever technical knowledge the United States has to the developing nations. AID, as the principal component in the United States technical cooperation program, is primarily concerned with the exchange of technical advice and professional competencies.

Advisory assistance is more than an exercise in diplomatic relations. Even though the adviser's role has obvious diplomatic overtones, the major emphasis in his work is upon professional responsibility rather than upon matters of diplomacy. This means that his advice has to be unselfish, hard-hitting, and culturally realistic. For this reason, it is important that the work of a community development adviser be primarily technically competent and professionally responsible and only secondarily politically popular.

A third element in advisory assistance is the identification of unsolved problems. It is one thing for the community development adviser to recognize that an emerging nation has problems, but it is quite another thing to reduce these problems conceptually to a level where they can be solved. Only when this is done can the next step, which is the separation of the major problems from the minor ones in order to establish priorities, be handled.

In many cases, new nations either attempt to solve all their problems at once, which usually means that none are solved; or they set out to solve minor problems which are not as important to their national development as others they might select. For instance, many nations build large national airway systems before they strengthen their political institutions. Restraint and clearheadness are required of the national leaders of these nations to choose problems for immediate solution which in the long run will contribute appreciably to the development of their nations.

AID is committed to this concept: when a major problem is identified, its solution is best approached through a series of short-term goals which can be achieved within a reasonable length of time. This concept has been successfully embodied in India's Five-Year Plans. In these plans, goals are clearly established and reasonably fixed so that meeting them does not take on that air of impossibility which so often leads to a sense of failure and finally to a loss of interest.

What this means is that a problem has to be phrased in specific rather than in general terms; its solution has to make a substantial contribution to the over-all development of the country; and the solution has to be sought in steps that are relatively easy to attain in a short period of time. It is not so much the existence of the problem that is important as it is the manner in which the problem is identified and the way in which the solutions are approached.

Another element in AID's definition of advisory assistance is the temporary nature of the adviser's work. The ultimate purpose of advisory assistance is to create a situation in which the recipient nation no longer needs outside assistance. Although no correlation has been found between the brevity of the advisory relationship and its success, long-term advisory relationships are discouraged. The temporary nature of the assistance provided is emphasized throughout the entire life of an advisory relationship so that the advisees are continually aware that ultimately they must stand on their own feet.

Another characteristic of advisory assistance is the adviser's position as an outsider. This characteristic is sometimes forgotten in the actual conduct of an advisory role. While the adviser has to be as familiar as it is humanly possible with the culture, the people, and the institutions with which he works, his role is always that of an outsider. He is called upon for assistance because he has skills, attitudes, or knowledge which the receiving country does not have but needs. The adviser is outside the culture in his knowledge, skills, and attitudes to begin with; and he has to continue outside the culture in order to maintain the perspective, the objectivity, and the neutrality he will lose if he becomes too intimately identified with the host country. Mainly, he has to remain outside the hierarchical power system he is advising. Just as it is possible to be too far away from a system to really understand it, it is equally possible to be too close to maintain a proper perspective of it.

There are no clear-cut rules that an adviser can use as guidelines to determine the distance he ought to maintain from the system he is advising. However, the experience of many technicians suggests that, while a technician never can know too much about the group he is helping, there is always the danger that he will become so much a part of the group that he will cease to be of value to it.

These five characteristics -- a voluntary association, professional assistance, the existance of an unsolved problem, a temporary relationship, and the necessity of having an outsider as an adviser -- summarize the major elements in AID's definition of advisory assistance. These characteristics by no means complete the meaning of advisory assistance; much more experience has to be accumulated before that can be done. However, they do provide a solid working basis upon which to analyze the role of the adviser, approaches to advisory assistance, and the educational aspects of advisory assistance.

THE ROLE OF THE ADVISER[3]

An adviser must bring to his overseas assignment a systematic analytic theory which enables him to select what to study and how to understand what he sees. Lippitt tells us that the adviser has to have a system of ideas or a concept to provide a framework for his perception of the things going on in the institution. This enables the adviser to make a decision about the nature of the group and to theorize about what makes the group behave the way it does. There are both advantages and disadvantages in having such a theory. Those with a theory -- whether it is a psychoanalytic theory, a learning theory, a social conflict theory, or a role theory -- have a much easier job in settling down to the business of giving advice because they have the means for organizing and comprehending what they see. On the other hand, these same people have a harder time in noticing and interpreting important events which are not taken into account by their theory. This, of course, is a major disadvantage.

In addition to having a systematic analytic theory, the adviser also needs a diagnostic theory to enable him to determine what has to be corrected. A diagnostic theory helps an adviser to detect the problem areas and to explain the causes for the pattern of symptoms. There are many possible diagnostic theories. For instance, in community development the range includes:

1. Too much power concentration on the national level and not enough on the village level.

2. Lack of communication among the various levels and the ministries involved in the program.

3. Inadequacy of decision-making and action-taking skills among the staff.

4. Personnel poorly trained in the purposes and the techniques of community development.

These and other theories about the nature of an institution's problems provide a device for a community development adviser to find sufficient information to identify the nature of the institution's problems and to make decisions about the kinds of help needed. In addition, the adviser's diagnostic theory helps him determine the direction in which improvement has to proceed.

Unfortunately, no one theory explains all problems. Therefore, a rigorous devotion to any one theory cannot be justified; instead, there has to be a readiness among advisers to consider other theories when special conditions call for a change.

In addition to a systematic analytic theory and a diagnostic theory, the community development adviser also has to know how to analyze forces of resistance and change. The adviser, like the village-level worker, is an agent of cultural change. At every stage in the development of his concept of what has to be changed and how it has to be changed, the adviser has to be alert to all those forces which encourage and resist change. There are times when an adviser has to desist from making a change and other times when he has to manipulate the conditions to create a favorable environment for change. All of these activities call for a penetrating knowledge of change and resistance forces.

This skill is outside and beyond the technical skill the adviser brings to the host country. On occasion, those responsible for hiring advisers mistakenly place primary emphasis upon the technical aspects of advisory work and neglect other, more important elements. For this reason, many advisers do not make a substantial contribution to the countries they are sent to assist.

If all the cooperating countries needed were additional

knowledge and skills, books could be sent to them in the
fields where they are deficient; and this would suffice. However, what they require is advice on the implementation of
this knowledge in their own cultures. This calls for the
employment of advisers with nontechnical as well as technical knowledge and skills. This nontechnical knowledge
includes, among other things, a systematic analytic theory,
a diagnostic theory, and the ability to handle the forces of
change and resistance.

The three factors just described are ones the community development adviser has to possess before he arrives in
the nation he is employed to assist. The next four factors to
be discussed represent skills the adviser has to work out in
the advisory situation. First, the adviser has to establish a
rapport with the groups who best represent the thinking of the
institution he is to change and who can bring about the required changes. An adviser has to know whether the people
he is in contact with speak for themselves, for a small sub-
group, or for the institution which employs them. Many advisers discover, sometimes too late, that their contacts,
even though official, are not part of the power structure and,
thus, are not in a position to really know what is going on or to
affect change.

An adviser's success depends upon his ability to bring
about change. But unless he is in contact with the major
change agents in any given institution, he cannot bring about
change. This places the establishment of contact with key
people at the forefront of the adviser's early strategy in an
advisory assistance program. Often this means that the
adviser has to work with the representatives of numerous
formal and informal groupings in an institution in order to
learn about all the operational patterns of the system.

This calls for a long period of systematic analysis
before the adviser can give advice. A good rule of thumb,
according to James Green, is for the adviser to spend
"ninety per cent of his time systematically learning and ten
per cent advising."[4] In the investigation of the behavioral
patterns of the group, the adviser has to discover what each
member of the group does, how he does it, when he does it,
where he does it, why he does it, and with whom he does it.
Only when he knows these things is he able to discover the
key people and the channels through which change can be

realized.   This kind of knowledge is particularly important when the adviser finally sits down to help a group clarify its problems and select appropriate solutions.

When the point is r e a c h e d where the problems are clarified, the diagnosis has been given, and the recommendations have been made, m a n y c o m m u n i t y development advisers feel that their task is finished.   However, the developing nations usually prove to be incapable of implementing the recommendations without further technical help from the adviser.   It is at this stage that the adviser has to shift from the nondirective role of helping the group develop and clarify its goals for change to the more active directive role of helping the group learn the procedures and skills necessary to work effectively toward the established goals.

Community development advisers in AID find they have to shift from the diagnostic role appropriate to the earlier phases of the advisory process to the more active training role which is necessary for the successful completion of the advisory assistance program.   Without this f i n a l training phase, the e n t i r e process of advisory assistance loses its long-range effectiveness.   The group being assisted requires training in the procedures of instituting change before they can set the machinery for change into motion.

Change is never easy, and most institutions are not adept in achieving it.   The old ways are the known ways, the comfortable ways, and the secure ways, and, thus, are not ways that are easily changed.   People have to be educated for change.   This training for change is the final and perhaps the most important p h a s e of the work community development advisers find themselves doing.

Obviously, a technical adviser is more than a technician with a facility for spotting w e a k points and offering advice on how these problem areas can be corrected.   He is also an educator who has to train the group he is working with in the skills and procedures necessary for correcting its problems.

APPROACHES TO ADVISORY ASSISTANCE

Not all technicians define technical assistance and its major component, advisory assistance, in quite the s a m e way. Most of the advisers in AID look upon themselves as consultant-trainers. However, even among this group there is divided opinion as to the exact role of the adviser. Some feel that the role of the adviser is to transmit skills, knowledge, and attitudes only. Others believe that institution building should be added to this basic training function.

There are two other concepts of advisory assistance. One is the practitioner concept, and the other is the pure consultant concept. Neither, however, has made much of an impact among advisers who have worked for AID and its predecessor agencies.

The Practitioner

Advisers who look upon advisory assistance as the performance of a specific operation are called practitioners. They believe that their primary assignment is to substitute for a local technician in the direct performance of some function. In some cases it involves a doctor treating patients on a village level and in others an engineer building a water system for a town. On occasion, the technician trains subordinates; but he never trains a replacement in the fullest sense. Often, there are incidental training activities, which are inevitable. However, the training of a local technician to replace the outside technician is never a major purpose.

The practitioner entertains no expectations that, as a result of his activities, the local people will carry on his work after he leaves. The assistance is entirely short-term and is not at all directed to the transmission of knowledge, attitudes, or skills. The educational aspects of this approach are so minimal that it is doubtful whether this approach should be classified in the general category of advisory assistance at all. [5]

The Consultant

The second approach to advisory assistance is that of the consultant. This role centers around consultation rather than the performance of actual operations. Consultants look upon their roles as that of diagnosing problems and making recommendations for change. This approach generally is nondirective and is not especially successful in developing nations where it is used. This is because the initiative, the skills, and the resources of the local staff usually are not sufficient to implement the recommendations offered. [6]

The consultant's approach to advisory assistance, like that of the practitioner's, places little or no emphasis upon educational activities. Training is completely ignored, and education is not valued as a significant part of the consultant's work.

The approaches of the practitioner and the consultant obviously do not have the scope nor the intensity of purpose needed to fulfill the expectations newly developing nations place in advisory assistance. Fortunately, neither has earned more than token support or passing mention by those who have worked for AID and its predecessor agencies.

The Consultant-Trainer[7]

The third approach, that of consultant-trainer, gives the closest attention to the role of education in advisory assistance. Also, it is the approach most widely supported by the community development advisers working for AID.

Those who support the consultant-trainer approach generally fall into one of two general categories. In one category are those who focus upon the transfer of skills, of knowledge, and of techniques to individuals and to groups. These advisers place a great amount of emphasis upon the training of nationals to do work that would otherwise have to be done by outsiders. The training is conducted either in the national's home country, in the United States, or in a third country. Those selected for training outside their home countries are called "participants."

Although participant training is very popular, it often falls short of achieving its basic purposes. One of the major weaknesses of sending nationals out of their own country for participant training is that they are removed from the specific day-to-day operational problems of the institution they are expected to change when they return. As a result, their attitudes and skills are sometimes changed without reference to what is going on in their home country.

Because of these limitations, the current view is that as much training as possible should be conducted within the institution where the individual works. This represents an alternate approach to the one in which selected individuals are trained in outside cultures and is offered as a more effective means of overcoming some of the obstacles to planned change built into the first methods.

This approach emphasizes the adviser's role as trainer as well as consultant. As a consultant, the adviser gives aid in the diagnosis of problems and the formulation of workable solutions. As a trainer, he helps his advisees acquire the knowledge and skill necessary to bring about the changes that are required. The focus of this training, unlike that received by participants in other cultures, is specifically directed to the problems which confront the staff. An important outcome of this approach is the way in which each of the involved staff members becomes aware of how others perceive existing problems and participate in the formulation of solutions for them. This increases the staff's skill in working cooperatively with others to bring about change on a broad scale. [8]

Another group of advisers who support the consultant-trainer approach add institution building to the training function. For them, advisory assistance is not merely the diagnosis of problems and the training of local people to solve problems, but, in addition, is the creation and the strengthening of the institutions required to solve these problems.

This approach is based upon the assumption that new nations not only lack knowledge, but also lack the organizational structures necessary for the implementation of new knowledge. The experience of nationals trained at home and of participants trained outside of their own cultures is used to substantiate this view. Nationals trained at home find they cannot put their learning to use once the advisers leave. And participants, upon returning home, find there are no institutions where they can implement their new learnings. These difficulties and disappointments strengthen the idea that institution building should be incorporated into the formal definition of advisory assistance.

Of the three approaches -- that of the practitioner, the consultant, and the consultant-trainer--the consultant-trainer concept appears to have the most meaning in terms of the demands placed upon community development advisers working

in developing nations. And the definition of consultant-trainer
which seems to have the most relevance is the one which adds
the function of institution building to the basic advisory assistance functions of diagnosis of the problems, recommendations
for change, and training.

THE ADVISER AS AN EDUCATOR

Every community development adviser brings a specific
technical or professional competency to the culture he advises.
This proficiency is ordinarily in a field related to public administration, education, or agriculture. However, the extent
of an adviser's value to an assisted country is not altogether
determined by the depth of his technical knowledge. The level
of technical knowledge many of the developing nations a r e
capable of implementing is low enough that many advisers find
themselves technically overeducated rather than undereducated
for their work. The final measure of an adviser's value is
usually his ability to transmit technical knowledge. The mere
possession of technical knowledge, then, is less of an asset
than the adviser's ability to communicate it.

However, the adviser has more to do than communicate
technical k n o w l e d g e as such. If this is all that is required, the adviser could record all the known knowledge in a
given field and send it to the country requesting aid. The
developing countries want more than this. More specifically,
they want the adviser to transmit the most appropriate items
of knowledge at a pace that is consistent with the needs and
the ability of the people in the culture to absorb it.

For this reason, before the adviser can transmit knowledge, attitudes, and skills, he has to study all aspects of the
society he is working with and, in particular, the institutions
where he wants to affect changes. This is a slow, tedious
and frequently frustrating task; but it is necessary because it
is the only way in which an adviser can determine what knowledge and skills to transmit.

Unless the adviser is able to convey to the officials of
the country where he is working a sense of the logic of his
diagnosis and can provide them with the skills and the procedures necessary to carry through the changes he recom-
mends, he indeed offers advice -- but he does not give assistance. The full process of advisory assistance is not complete

until that which is transmitted is received; and, when this happens, the processes of education take place.

Whenever a community d e v e l o p m e n t adviser or any other kind of adviser is able to convince a government official to change a particular procedure or to reexamine the organization of his department, then educational processes a r e necessarily at work.

Community development advisers achieve these changes in a number of ways. These include short courses, conferences and seminars, and the day-to-day contacts the adviser has with officials. Many of these techniques require formal teaching because teaching enables the adviser to b r i n g together large numbers and a greater cross section of officials than he can reach on a more informal basis. In this way, the adviser is able to involve people at all levels within an institution and, thereby, widen his scope of influence.

In his teaching role, the adviser aims to make himself dispensable. He strives to train others to do the teaching he is currently doing. In order to achieve this, community development advisers make every effort to work through t h e instructors, the development officers, and the administrators of the national community development programs in the countries where they work.

Many years ago, Charlotte Towle, a well-known social worker and educator, found that teaching was one of the biggest responsibilities the adviser has. [9] She discovered that the adviser's teaching role includes b o t h structured classroom teaching and on-the-spot informal teaching activities. The experience of United States community development personnel certainly confirms Miss Towle's findings. They find that the role of education in advisory assistance is not peripheral, but is an integral part of their task. This, of course, has implications for the recruitment, selection, and training of community development advisers. Unfortunately, AID and its predecessor agencies have never fully explored these implications in terms of their own activities.

Since education plays such a vital part in the adviser's work, selection criteria for advisers must go beyond technical competency. Selection must also be based upon an applicant's ability to communicate knowledge, attitudes, and skills because, over the long run, ability in this area plays as great a, if not greater, part as technical competency ensuring effectiveness.

Training is so much a part of the adviser's work that he should come to this task equipped with a viable philosophy of education. This philosophy should include an awareness of the importance of action-oriented teaching programs rather than subject-matter–based programs, an appreciation of the need to keep training as close as possible to the situation for which the trainees are being prepared, and a commitment to the principle that training has to be flexible and adjustable to meet changing needs. [10]

Proficiency is a by-product of training; and, if an adviser is to grow professionally, he has to receive careful training in teaching techniques throughout his professional career. His role as an educator demands a special understanding of human behavior and how it can be changed. It also necessitates a broad knowledge of the learning processes and their application to teaching situations. In addition, since people respond to the educational media that capture and hold their attention, the adviser has to be equipped with skills in handling audio-visual aids. Finally, since much of the adviser's teaching has to be done through groups, the adviser should be adept in planning and leading group discussions. [11]

CONCLUSION

This chapter examined the educational aspects of one of the most important functions performed by AID personnel: advisory assistance. The educational implications were highlighted in the discussions of the definition of advisory assistance, the role of the adviser, and the approaches to advisory assistance, and, finally, summarized in the section dealing with the adviser as an educator.

Neither AID nor its predecessor agencies were ever fully aware of the full range of educational processes involved in advisory assistance activities. This was not an intentional oversight; rather, the reason was much less deliberate. The staff responsible for community development operations was so preoccupied with developing a philosophy and the procedures for community development in the new nations that it all but ignored the full analysis of its own role within the framework of a government a g e n c y supporting community development programs on an international scale. As a result, the community development s t a f f formulated an excellent theory of community development for the newer nations, but never constructed a series of adequate guidelines for implementing the theories it formulated.

NOTES TO CHAPTER 5

[1] The definition of advisory assistance used in this chapter is based upon the one used by Ronald Lippitt in "Dimensions of the Consultant's Job, " The Journal of Social Issues, XV (1959), 5-12.

[2] Cited by the National Education Association, Educational Policies Commission, Point Four and Education (Washington, D. C.: The Association, 1950), p. 1.

[3] Lippitt, loc. cit.

[4] James W. Green, "Guidelines to the Role of ICA-Aid Advisors, " quoted in class notes for "Application of Sociology to Problems of Rural Society, Rural Sociology 218, " Summer, 1958, Cornell University, Ithaca, N. Y. Copy found on file in the library of the Community Development Division, ICA, Washington, D. C.

[5] Gustav Papanek, Framing a Development P r o g r a m (New York: International Conciliation, Carnegie Endowment for International Peace, 1960), pp. 344-45.

[6] Charles Seashore and Elmer Van Egmond, "The Consultant Trainer Role in Working Directly with the Total Staff, " The Journal of Social Issues, XV (1959), 36-38.

[7] Papanek, loc. cit.

[8] Seashore and Van Egmond, loc. cit.

[9] As quoted by Ruth Gilbert, "Functions of the Consultant, " Teachers College Record, LXI (January, 1960), 185.

[10] Gordon L. Lippitt, "Consulting with a National Organization: A Case Study, " The Journal of Social Issues, XV (1959), 25.

[11] John M. Fenley (ed.), "Improving Personnel Training in Rural Development, " Mimeo Release 2 (Ithaca, N. Y.: Cornell University, 1960), pp. 27–30.

CHAPTER **6** THE ROLE OF
TRAINING IN
COMMUNITY
DEVELOPMENT

AID and its predecessor agencies have given vigorous support to training programs for all levels of community development personnel. Training, according to one community development staff member, is the key factor in the community development picture.[1] This attention to training goes back to the early days of United States involvement in community development programs overseas. In 1953, the Technical Cooperation Administration, a predecessor agency of AID, placed the training of indigenous community development workers at the forefront of all of its activities.[2] In implementing this principle, the United States has a strong ally in the British, who have long recognized that training is an indispensable means of building effective community development programs.

The importance of formalized training is not appreciated by everyone in the field of community development. Isabel Kelly believes that adequate performance on the part of the village worker is more a matter of personality than of training.[3] Others who share Miss Kelly's view cite examples of community development program leaders and people on the village level who are able to change without the benefit of extensive training programs. However, Miss Kelly and those who share her views represent a small minority.

Those who defend training argue that the gap between community development methods and the cultural patterns of the areas where the methods have to be implemented is generally so great that well-organized training schemes are required. This point is usually demonstrated by citing the great difficulties faced by those who attempt to foster the use of democratic values and processes on the village level. These values do not exist in most tradition-bound village situations where people have been told for centuries what to do and, through bitter experience, have come to look upon the government as an enemy rather than as a friend or a partner.

Before these cultural patterns can be altered, changes

have to occur within the civil servants who deal with villagers as representatives of the government. Civil servants, as a rule, are not easy to change because the traditional system grants them much more security and status than the new system will ever give them. Thus, success in changing village people is not achieved casually or offhandedly, but requires highly organized training programs.

Those who stress the value of training argue further that a village-level worker is an agent of change. This means that, in addition to performing technical tasks, he functions as an expert in human relations. He has to know how to organize groups, lead discussions, and plan committee meetings. These skills are difficult to learn and usually acquired only in training programs especially designed to develop them.

There is an additional element which is often mentioned in discussions on training. National community development programs demand a cross-country uniformity in philosophy and practice. No matter how perceptive a community development worker is, there is no way, except a systematic training program, for him to fully appreciate such items as the lines of communication of the organization, government policy and procedure, and the technical services available through the program. Training also is needed to increase the sense of unity among the staff as well as its sense of being part of a large and important profession, qualities which are necessary for a worker's initial confidence and continuing success in his work.

TRAINING ADMINISTRATIVE AND TECHNICAL PERSONNEL

AID and its predecessor agencies have always placed strong emphasis upon training local citizens and village-level workers. This emphasis makes sense because training at these levels unquestionably is a crucial factor in the over-all effectiveness of community development programs.

However, the agency's case for training does not stop on the village level. It includes as well a provision for training persons in technical and administrative posts above the village level whose work is related to community development. Unfortunately, in many countries, this level of training is neglected. Robert Polson found that the training of higher echelon program administrators with supervisory responsibility related to community development programs is one of the most neglected areas of training. [4]

Training arrangements for administrative staff are important because the establishment of a functioning community development program calls for an entirely new kind of public servant. Usually, community development departments are staffed with personnel from other trades and professions. This means that, before they can function as effective administrators, they have to be schooled in the purposes, the procedures, and even the role of community development in the nation-building process.

Community development has its own set of values, concepts, and principles; and these are quite distinct from those of any other program. For instance, the village-level multipurpose worker is a social technician, a culture innovator, and an agent of change. All these titles describe a worker who has to have a broad combination of technical and human-relation skills. The multipurpose worker's specialty, says Durham, is generalized skill. [5]

This concept constitutes not only new but radical thinking for both village-level workers and technical and administrative personnel in the higher levels of the government. In addition to being new and radical, this idea runs counter to the basic philosophy and procedures of many of the governments that hope to foster community development on a broad scale. Hence, government administrators have to undergo a fundamental change in their own thinking and acquire a new set of tools and a new philosophy in order to carry out the objectives of community development.

Another reason for training administrators is that the ultimate success of a community development program depends upon the administrative support it receives from government officials. It has been found that where government officials, through misunderstanding, oppose or mishandle a program, it is only a matter of time before the program collapses.

However, it is not easy to construct effective training programs for personnel at this level. For one thing, it means retraining. Since all of the administrators and the technicians were trained once, they often feel that they do not need additional training. Also, many administrators, particularly those who hold highly responsible positions, have little time for extensive retraining.

In spite of these and other problems, many administrators receive training. The training usually consists of short conferences and seminars. On occasion, field trips to village programs are used. In addition, efforts are made to have articles on community development published in the periodicals and newspapers that are read by government administrators. And a few administrators in each country are selected for participant training in the United States or a third country.

One of the most neglected yet potentially fruitful training resources for administrators is the university. Wherever it is utilized, the university lends prestige to the community development movement and makes the training program much more attractive to prospective trainees. In some countries, the universities devise training programs that include studies of the nature and the scope of community development and its place in the political, economic, and social planning of the government, skill training in working with individuals and groups, and the effective communication of ideas. [6]

The reports of those who have reviewed community development programs in the field nearly always contain references to the great need for training administrative personnel. S. C. Dube, in reporting on India's community development program, says that government officials completely ignore democratic values and processes, tend to plan from the top down, and treat villagers as subordinates rather than as partners in a cooperative program to secure national development. [7] His report supports the view that the traditional ways of thinking are so persistent that intensive orientation and inservice training programs are an absolute necessity if the values of government officials are ever to be changed.

Dube's observations are confirmed by the experience of another community development specialist, Carl C. Taylor. After a close study of a number of programs, he reported that there was a need for consciously trained administrators to provide leadership in general community development. The skills he describes as important for administrators are those generally associated with the fields of community organization, rural sociology, and adult education. [8]

Over the years, few of the national community development programs supported by United States funds have created adequate training programs for administrative personnel. India comes closest to achieving this goal than any other country. India provides training for block, district, state, and regional community development personnel as well as for development commissioners who meet at a yearly commissioners' conference.

This extensive provision for training is one of the most outstanding characteristics of India's program. The training of the state and national officials through seminars and conferences and the more structured training of community development specialists and subject area specialists on all levels are built into the everyday functioning of India's community development program.

In addition to special training programs for administrative personnel, the United States also stresses training for the technical specialists who support the work of the community development personnel. The specialists' general misunderstanding of the goals of community development, their feeling that community development duplicates and, thereby, threatens their own programs, and their sense of competition with community development workers cause them to be a disrupting rather than a supporting element in the community development programs of many countries.

For these reasons, the United States has encouraged countries, such as the Philippines, to train these technicians. At the lower levels, there have been successful experiments in the training of technical workers along with multipurpose workers. Joint classes have been organized in group dynamics, communications, and agricultural economics. Through studying together and building a common base of knowledge, it has been found that they can work together without the institutional rivalry which has up until now characterized their relationships.

Senior technical officers have slightly different training programs because of time and prestige factors. Instead of attending long sessions, they participate in council meetings, briefing sessions, seminars, and observation tours.

The training of administrative and technical personnel

at all levels within both community development departments and divisions whose activities support and relate to national community development programs is given top priority by the United States community development staff. It recognizes that, without training at these levels, the unity of approach and the understanding of community development that is a prerequisite for effective programs cannot be achieved.

TRAINING VILLAGE-LEVEL MULTIPURPOSE WORKERS

One of the most significant contributions the United States has made in the field of community development is the support it has given to the development of a viable training philosophy for multipurpose village-level workers. The important aspects of this philosophy are: first, the use of village experience and facility in the language of the region as major criteria for selecting trainees for village work; second, the provision for the active participation of the trainees in all learning experiences; third, training in practical as well as human relations skills; and fourth, frequent in-service and refresher courses after the initial orientation program.

There are many factors which have not proved to be too important in determining the success or failure of village-level workers. Age is certainly one such factor. Carl C. Taylor reports that in India village boys with no more and sometimes less than a high school education are accepted by the villagers and do as commendable a job as much older workers. [9]

It is more difficult to generalize about the amount of education a village worker needs. Isabel Kelly says that in India they need just enough education to enable them to establish rapport with the people of a village and to speak with sufficient authority to command respect. [10] On the other hand, community development leaders in the Philippines believe that a village worker needs a college degree.

In actual fact, what works in the Philippines appears to have been ruinous in India. Dube, in reporting on India's program, says that, on the whole, university graduates have not proved to be successful as village-level workers. Their superior attitudes, manner of speech and dress, and constant desire for promotion to a higher post stand in the way of their applying themselves wholeheartedly to their jobs. [11]

While agreement has never been reached on the exact importance of age and educational background in the success of community development workers, there is no question about the importance of previous village experience and facility in the language of the local region. Almost all community development training centers list knowledge of a regional language and village background or experience as specific entrance requirements for the training program. The relationship of the multipurpose worker to the villagers he works with has to be built upon understanding and confidence. The knowledge of villagers that comes from village living and from speaking with villagers in their own language are indispensable sources of this understanding and confidence.

The second aspect of the United States philosophy of training is the belief that the best teaching techniques are those which allow the learner to participate in the learning experience. Field work, demonstration methods, and learning by doing replace the lecture and the textbook approach; and a strong emphasis is placed upon informal methods which the trainees can use in their village work.

India provides outstanding examples of the use of practical work in her training programs. In 1957, for instance, at the Himayatsagar Extension Training Center, there were no textbooks; and each trainee worked to a problem-oriented syllabus with detailed notes specially prepared by the instructor for intensive practical training. From one half to as much as two thirds of the trainee's class time in any given subject was spent at the center's farm and in village fields where the trainee learned by doing. [12]

Different training centers in India have different schedules of field work, but all have field work. Some send trainees to villages for field experiences on alternate months, with the months in between spent in lectures and discussions. Others send trainees to the village for one week at a time; or, if they are close enough to the villages, they send half the trainees out in the morning and the other half out in the afternoon.

The emphasis upon the practical in India's training programs is not only reflected in teaching methods, but also in course content. In 1960, at the Himachal Pradesh Extension Training Center, the subject matter of courses in the field included plowing, sowing, harvesting, first aid practices, spraying and dusting fields, improvement of roads, sanitation, and castration of bulls. And in the villages, the course work included conducting discussion groups, digging manure pits, laying out demonstration plots, improving the drinking water supply, and flash-card talks. [13]

The practicality of the training is an important factor in the choice of sites for training centers. Sites are selected which offer good facilities for supervised field experience under realistic conditions. For this reason, the training of multipurpose workers is generally conducted in rural areas and as close as possible to the villages where the trainees are to return when they complete their training. [14]

Another element in the training philosophy deals with the training of multipurpose workers in human relations skills. These skills are called by a variety of names: core content, social content, extension techniques, and the educational approach to service. [15]

The case for teaching human relations skills in a community development program is an easy one to plead. The forces that multipurpose workers have to work with in order to bring about change are human forces. These include the local people, government officials, and members of the appropriate technical and professional groups.

An apt description of the community development worker's primary role can be found in the term "innovator of change." His dual objective is to stimulate local people to participate more actively in the life of their nation and to work toward a higher standard of living. Whenever people learn how to utilize local resources, and how to call upon the services of the national government to supplement their own activities, changes occur. Human change, then, is the goal of village-level workers; and, to achieve it, they have to exercise a set of skills beyond those normally possessed by an agriculturalist, a health worker, or an engineer.

If a multipurpose worker is to be effective, he has to learn how to use organized groups to promote village action, how to obtain the participation of citizens in cooperative activities, and how to use discussion groups and planning committees. These are all human development activities that community development workers have to become adept in using.

In addition to training in human relations skills, trainees for village-level work are given technical training. Proficiency in practical subjects is a basic requirement for success as a village-level worker. No one is more aware of this than the workers themselves. When interviewed and asked what studies could have been dealt with in greater detail in their preservice training programs, the interviewees answered that they would have liked more work in technical subjects. Those interviewed expressed an interest in acquiring more skill practice in the identification and control of common plant and animal diseases, the marketing of the products of cottage industries, training in the economics of small projects in poultry and pigs, and agricultural practice for rice terraces.[16]

Multipurpose village-level workers require a special kind of technical training. Their training is essentially different than that of those training to work exclusively in one of the technical fields, such as agriculture, health, or education. The key difference is that a multipurpose worker receives elementary training in a number of fields, whereas an ordinary technician is highly trained in only one field. The multipurpose worker is a generalist rather than a specialist who approaches every problem he encounters as one which has to be solved in terms of many fields rather than just one. For this reason, the multipurpose worker is trained to render first aid service in the wide number of fields which touch upon the everyday living experiences of villagers.

The concept of the multipurpose worker as it is defined by United States community development personnel does not rule out the need for technical specialists on the village level. As a matter of fact, it encourages the more efficient use of technical specialists. The multipurpose worker is expected to call upon technical specialists when the problems he faces demand a greater technical competency than he possesses. In doing this, the multipurpose worker is able to integrate government technical services on the village level and to correct the tendency of the separate technical departments to operate in isolation of one another.

Another important aspect of the training philosophy for multipurpose workers is the belief that the initial preservice training program should be followed by in-service training. Actually, this is the weakest part of many community development programs supported by the United States. This is due largely to the shortage of personnel in the field of community development. There are simply not enough training personnel to guide village workers in the field. In addition, most countries are so occupied with building and maintaining a preservice training program that they never reach the stage where they can afford to give much attention to in-service training.

The United States believes that training village-level personnel is an ongoing function which has to be provided throughout the entire career of the worker. The ever-expanding body of research on matters related to community development, the poor training many village-level workers receive initially, and the need to recapture the initial enthusiasm many workers lose in the course of the daily failure and frustration they meet in their work has motivated the United States to encourage the growth of in-service programs for all field workers in national community development programs.

The principal methods recommended for supplementing the original preservice training all village-level workers receive are supervision, in-service training, and refresher courses. In addition, many countries are experimenting with the use of publications which are regularly distributed to all field personnel. Where this latter technique is used, it has proved to be an important means of keeping field workers apprised of the newest ideas in community development. Usually, these publications contain articles on policy and procedure in community development, success stories of workers in the field, and case histories.

THE TRAINING OF VILLAGE-LEVEL LEADERS

The publications of United States community development staff members contain numerous references to the importance of training village-level leaders. For the most part, the training is thought of as the informal, unstructured, day-to-day interaction between a multipurpose worker and local villagers. However, there is a growing appreciation of the value of a more formalized type of training for local leaders. In the early days of her national program, India established training camps for local leaders to stimulate their interest and to elicit their cooperation. Over the years, these camps

have moved toward increasingly specialized courses. Mainly,
these camps have evolved a training program that is geared
to preparing the local leaders in technical subjects so that
they can go back to their homes to institute reform and to
assist the multipurpose workers.

The best training programs are those which do not draw
the local leaders too far away from the life of their communities, are of short duration, give the trainees an opportunity
to work with experienced local leaders, and are conducted by
the multipurpose workers and technicians assigned to the
trainees' home areas. By starting on a foundation of the familiar, local leaders are brought with greater ease and effectiveness to the unfamiliar.

The Philippines conducts an all-out program to train
and develop local leaders at lay training institutes. Ramon P.
Binamira, one-time presidential assistant on community development in the Philippines, looks upon the training of village
leaders as an important means of developing effective and
dynamic local leadership. In addition, he believes this training is a valuable method of strengthening the barrio council as
a unit of action for community development, of making the
council an effective unit of local government, and of establishing working relations between the people and the government
agencies concerned with community development. [17] The experience of the Philippines shows that the traditional concept
of training community development workers has to be expanded
to include the indigenous volunteer village leaders if community development programs are to achieve their full potential.

Of special note here is the Comilla Cooperative Project
in East Pakistan, which began in early 1960, as an experiment within the framework of the Basic Democracy Program to find out why the village-AID program had been unsuc-
cessful and to find a better approach to community development.
The project made a break from the pattern of community development started in India in 1952. It replaced the paid multipurpose worker with trained village leaders selected by the
village people. Also, it administered the program of rural
development through the existing administrative organization
of governments rather than through new administrative units.

Ernest Neal sees this as part of a larger trend to shift
to local governing bodies many of the functions previously

assigned to the multipurpose worker, to improve the competency and the number of personnel in the technical ministries,
and to relegate community workers to trainers of local governing bodies. [18]

THE TRAINING PROGRAM IN THE PHILIPPINES FOR COMMUNITY DEVELOPMENT WORKERS

In 1958, Paul Philips reported to the Washington office
of the Community Development Division of ICA that the community development program in the Philippines:

> . . . most nearly approached the ideal for impact
> and participation, that it gave major emphasis to
> self help, and made maximum use of locally con-
> tributed materials and labor and that the workers
> had excellent training and orientation which en-
> abled them to operate effectively on the village
> level. [19]

His comment reflects the views of many other community development specialists who have observed the Philippine community development program.

A good part of the success of the Philippine program
is a result of the emphasis it gives to the role of training.
Ramon Binamira believes that it is impossible to overempha-
size the importance of training in this new approach to nation-
building. [20]

The Philippines' training program d r e w ideas from
many sources. It is an outgrowth of a highly coordinated program of assistance given by the United Nations, the United
States, and the Philippine Government. Essentially, its development is an exercise in international education and its
success a testimonial to international cooperation. This coordinated help is largely responsible for the Philippines' use
of the broad-sweep theory of training community development
workers. In implementing this theory, the Philippines developed a preservice training program for prospective community development workers, in-service training for field workers, supervisory t r a i n i n g for supervisors, an orientation
program for technical department field workers and policy-
and decision-makers, and a lay leadership training program.

Specifically, the Philippine c o m m u n i t y development training program is conducted in five distinct, but closely co-ordinated, programs. The first is the six-month preservice course provided for prospective field workers. Those chosen for this program have to be graduates of a four-year college or have had two years of college education with two or more years' equivalent experience in community development work. Their program includes a sixteen-week basic training program in which they study community development as a concept, the role of g o v e r n m e n t in community development, group dymanics, rural sociology, agriculture, homemaking, and other practical skills. To this is a d d e d a six-week supervised field practice experience. Upon completion of the course, the trainees have to agree to serve at least two years as barrio c o m m u n i t y development workers in whatever barrios they are assigned.

The second type of training is that provided for supervisors, line workers, and other staff members through in-service training. Generally, it consists of either on-the-job training or short seminars, but also includes meetings, conferences, special duties, rotation of assignments, lectures, and special reading. These programs are operated on the principle that training has to be provided periodically throughout the worker's entire career.

The third type of training is that provided for the policy- and decision-makers of community development departments and technicians in cooperating departments. A r e l a t i v e l y short orientation program of six weeks, as compared to the six-month preorientation program provided for multipurpose workers, is given to the technical workers who support the activities of the multipurpose workers.

Since these w o r k e r s have adequate technical backgrounds, none of the course material in their training programs deals with technical skills. Instead, the courses are directed to the study of group d y n a m i c s, communication skills, community development concepts, public administration, rural sociology, agricultural economics, and coordination and teamwork.

Unfortunately, the training of policy and decision makers has never been as fully formalized. The training for policy-makers consists largely of council meetings, briefing sessions, seminars in community development, observation tours, and reports.

Another type of training program is that provided for barrio council members, civic and youth leaders, and other volunteers. Training for these lay leaders is conducted for varying lengths of time. However, it is rarely less than four days. Most of the training is conducted in small groups, and the laboratory approach is used wherein one problem is selected for each day of the training session. The unwritten tradition in these sessions is that there are to be no speeches or long lectures.

A unique type of training is provided for third-country participants from Southeast Asia, the Far East, and other parts of the world. The success of the community development program in the Philippines attracts many visitors who are anxious to secure ideas they can use in their own community development programs. The number of visitors has mounted year by year, until now it is almost impossible for the office of the PACD to program activities for third-country participants with any degree of proficiency.

All of these training programs are conducted at a special community development center and in the field. The center, which was called the Luzon Community Development Training Center until October 7, 1957, started operations with 342 preservice trainees on April 9, 1956.

In the first year and a half of its operations, the center was conducted as a joint undertaking of the College of Agriculture, the University of the Philippines, and the PACD; and it developed its curriculum under the guidance of the university faculty, the PACD staff, ICA and the UN advisers, and professors from Cornell University. In October of 1957, the name of the center was changed to Los Banos Community Development Center; and it was moved to a new building on the campus of the College of Agriculture at the University of the Philippines.

Los Banos serves as a center for preservice training, inservice training, and the orientation of technical support agency representatives, and as a site for seminars, workshops, conferences, and institutes. Its work is extensive and far-reaching. Between 1958 and 1960 alone, the center provided six-month in-service training programs for 1, 220, six-week orientation programs for 551, and in-service training for 168. [21]

Between 1956 and 1966, the training programs in the Philippines for all levels of community development workers were developed with the assistance of the United States, which provided American technicians, material support, and dollar aid.

Over this period, the validity of two very important hypotheses was substantiated. The first is that training is of vital importance for effective community development programs, and the second is that training must be provided for all community development personnel if programs are to achieve the consistency and coordination required for success.

COMMON FAILINGS IN COMMUNITY DEVELOPMENT TRAINING PROGRAMS

The four most common failings in the community development training programs supported by the United States are the neglect of sound educational principles, the limited amount of research and evaluation, the gap between the theories taught in the training centers and the realities of village life, and the indifference to in-service training.

When the issue of educational method is raised, many retort with a commentary on the value of subject matter. The central problem, however, is not really a matter of pure method or pure subject matter, but rather how can both be combined to achieve the best possible training program. The teaching of subject matter is always an important objective in training programs. However, its acquisition depends upon the methods used to transmit it. Therefore, both subject matter and method play an important role in training courses.

One major problem in many of the training programs is reflected in the way instructors define training objectives. Frequently, objectives are defined in terms of the performance of a number of routine tasks in the classroom rather than in terms of the tasks the trainee will face in his work situation. Many instructors fail to realize that the trainees need a body of skills and principles and that the sheer memorization of facts cannot give them the tools they need in village-level work.

For instance, much of the teaching done at the Community Training Institute in Pakistan in its early days was through lectures, a few demonstrations, a little supervised practical work, and examinations which stressed memorization and not the ability to perform. The institute sought to transfer knowledge and ideas, but not skills of either the technical or the human relations type. The result was that they produced village workers who were filled with facts, but unable to perform even the most elementary agricultural skill. Through a series of workshops and seminars, ICA advisers helped those teaching at the institute to change their attitudes and to shift the emphasis in their programs from pure lectures to skills instruction. [22]

United States community development personnel overseas believe that the purpose of training community development workers is to produce workers who are capable of using democratic teaching techniques in their work. This purpose, they find, is only achieved when democratic educational techniques are used in the training of workers themselves, because the techniques used in the training school establish the pattern that the trainee uses in his own work.

The second area of failure in many training programs is the neglect of research and evaluation. A continual evaluation of the content and the techniques of training programs is required in order to select the most pertinent subject matter out of which to build educational experiences that encourage learning. Research is needed to determine what constitutes the most relevant body of knowledge for a training institute, what skills have to be taught, and how the different subjects are to be timed and integrated.

In addition to the content and the procedures of instruction, research is needed on the recruitment and selection procedures for all community development positions in order to determine the proper methods of selecting qualified people. [23]

Another common failure is the great gap between the theories taught in the classroom and the realities of village life. Dube, in describing India's community development program, criticized the unrealistic idealism and overoptimism he found in its training program. He felt India would have made greater gains if it had sensitized the trainees to the realities of village life before sending them out to work. [24]

In interviewing village-level workers, Dube found that almost all workers thought that some aspect of their training was unrealistic. They reported that in their training courses they were taught that methods of work in community development programs would not follow traditional bureaucratic lines and that the relationship between village-level workers and higher project officials would not be a superior-subordinate relationship. Yet, when the workers went into the field, they found that the administrative structure was much the same as other government departments and that high-ranking officials came to the field to inspect them rather than to help them. [25]

Another fault the village workers cited was the unrealistic emphasis placed upon grass-roots planning in the training programs. Time and time again the trainees were told that the people on the village level should be stimulated to direct their own development. In reality, the village-level workers found that plans for village improvement invariably came from the top and that they were expected to impose the programs upon the villagers. Another gap the workers identified was in the area of technical support. The technical and administrative support they were told was theirs for the asking was seldom, if ever, available. [26]

Another failure in community development training programs is the limited opportunity for in-service training. Many workers feel that there should be more refresher courses. In addition, they express the need for an increased supply of magazines and pamphlets dealing with community development and written on a level that they can understand.

CONCLUSION

The United States, through countries it supported in the field of community development, helped pioneer a philosophy of training which is unparalleled in scope and purpose in the history of intergovernmental programs in community development. This philosophy is best described as a broad-sweep theory of training. It is founded on the assumption that training is a central element in successful community development programs. On the basis of this theory, training programs are constructed which provide, in varying degrees, for the formal and systematic training of all community development workers throughout their entire careers. Administrators, technical staff, multipurpose village-level workers, and local leaders are all trained in preservice, in-service orientation, and refresher courses.

NOTES TO CHAPTER 6

[1] R. V. Bernhart, memorandum to Paul D. Summers reporting on the Ceylon Conference on Community Development Training. Copy found in the country file, Community Development Division, ICA, Washington, D. C.

[2] United States Technical Cooperation Administration, Community Services Staff, "Methods of Obtaining Participation in Self-Help Activities" (Washington, D. C.: The Administration, 1953), p. 9.

[3] Isabel Kelly, "Some Community Development Ailments, Suggested Diagnosis and Therapy" (Washington, D. C.: Community Development Division, ICA, 1960), p. 29.

[4] Robert A. Polson, "Theory and Methods of Training for Community Development, " Rural Sociology, XXIII (March, 1958), 34.

[5] Arthur Durham, "The Outlook of Community Development: An International Symposium, " International Review of Community Development, V (1960), 49.

[6] United Kingdom, Colonial Office, Community Development--A Handbook (London: Her Majesty's Stationery Office, 1958), pp. 55-56.

[7] S. C. Dube, India's Changing Villages (Ithaca, N. Y.: Cornell University Press, 1958), p. 164.

[8] As cited by Durham, op. cit., 50.

[9] Carl C. Taylor, A Critical Analysis of India's Community Development Program (India: Community Projects Administration, 1956), p. 27.

[10]Kelly, op. cit., p. 18.

[11]Dube, op. cit., p. 171.

[12]United Nations, "Experiments in Training for Community Development" (New York: United Nations, 1957), pp. 7-9.

[13]Prem Sagar Sharma, "Training Extension Workers in India Who Have Not Had Agricultural College Training," in "Improving Personnel Training in Rural Development," ed. by John M. Fenley, Mimeo Release 2 (Ithaca, N. Y.: Cornell University, 1960), pp. 14-15.

[14]United Nations, Bureau of Social Affairs, Social Progress Through Community Development (New York: United Nations, 1955), p. 104.

[15]United Nations, Study Kit on Training for Community Development (New York: United Nations, 1957), p. 14.

[16]Robert A. Polson, "A Report on the Training Aspects of the Philippine Community Development Program" (Manila: ICA, 1960), pp. 5-6.

[17]Ramon P. Binamira, "Training Community Development Personnel and Voluntary Leaders," Aspects of National Community Development Programs in Asia, United Nations Series on Community Development (New York: United Nations, 1959), p. 52.

[18]Ernest Neal, "A Report on Community Development in the Philippines, East Pakistan and India" (Washington, D. C.: AID, 1964), pp. 12-13.

[19]Paul Philips, airgram from CINCREP, Seoul, Korea, June 13, 1958, reporting on the PACD program in the Philippines. Copy found in country files, Community Development Division, ICA, Washington, D. C.

[20]Binamira, loc. cit.

[21]Philippines, The President's Office, Presidential Assistant on Community Development, Training and the Community Development Center (Manila: The President's Office, n. d.), p. 2.

[22] James W. Green, "Rural Development in Pakistan; The Village Aid Program," Community Development Review, VI (September, 1957), 59.

[23] Dube, op. cit., p. 149.

[24] Ibid., p. 164.

[25] Ibid.

[26] Ibid., pp. 164–65, 171.

CHAPTER **7**

PARTICIPANT TRAIN-
ING FOR COMMUNITY
DEVELOPMENT PER-
SONNEL IN THE
UNITED STATES AND
THIRD COUNTRIES

People brought to the United States for study and travel under the auspices of AID are called "participants." They are given a small lapel pin to wear throughout their stay with the words "Sharing Technical Knowledge Through International Cooperation, USA Participant" inscribed around an engraving of two hands locked in friendship. The pin, in addition to summarizing the purposes of participant training, identifies the participants as they move about the United States.

Participant training has caught hold of the imagination of policy-makers in the American government and has become one of America's major activities in the field of international education. One government document refers to it as the key element in the technical and educational programs carried on between the United States and other countries.[1]

The program has grown rapidly. For instance, the number of participants brought to the United States in 1960 represented an increase of 5,000 over the number brought in 1950. Over 100,000 participants in all have been brought to the United States by AID and its predecessor agencies. The numbers in themselves are indicative of the vigor with which the United States supports participant training as an instrument of technical cooperation.

The phenomenon of studying in a country other than one's own is not new. As early as the classical Greek and Roman periods, students traveled to other nations to secure knowledge they could not receive at home. And the traveling scholar, going from one university center to another in the pursuit of new learning, was a common figure in educational circles during the Middle Ages. The travel of Americans to German universities in the late Nineteenth Century is another and more recent example of students seeking advanced training outside their own country.

What is new is the full-scale effort by a single nation,

the United States, to educate large numbers of students in cultures other than their own. In this sense, participant training represents a colossal effort in international education, unmatched in the history of mankind. The effect of training 100,000 leaders from every part of the globe, under the auspices of the United States, has yet to be fully determined. However, there is little doubt, especially among those who work with the participants, that the effect is far-reaching.

Participant training is mainly justified on the grounds that the educational institutions of the new nations, where the majority of participants come from, are inadequate. Those who object to participant training feel that this problem could be resolved in other ways. They feel that a better solution would be to send teachers from the developed nations to the needy countries to establish training institutions. This, they believe, would be less expensive and would make it easier to relate the training to the culture of the trainees.

Those who favor participant training rally around three basic arguments. First, they maintain that there are some educational experiences a participant can secure in the United States that he cannot receive in his home country. For example, participants learn the basic tenets of a capitalistic democratic society with greater ease in the United States than they ever could in their home countries.

Also, proponents feel that participants who study in America develop a deeper attachment to the United States than they would otherwise have. This argument is of great appeal to Congressional appropriation committees.

Thirdly, proponents agree that, in some fields, the number who require training is so small that it would be impractical to establish local training programs for them. For instance, in the Philippines, there is a need to train only a few people for executive positions in the fields of agricultural extension and community development program planning and evaluation. It is easier and, in the long run, less expensive to send a few trainees to other countries than it is to establish a training program for them at home.

While the debate continues, so does the stream of participants being brought to the United States for study in every field and from every part of the world. They train in the fields of agriculture, industry, transportation, labor, health, public safety, education, public administration, community development, social welfare, housing, a n d atomic energy; and they represent countries in the Far East, Latin America, the Near East, Europe, and Africa. Numerically, subject-fieldwise, and geographically, AID has a diversified program that has no parallel in history.

In 1955, the Community Development Division of ICA, as a unit within the technical cooperation p r o g r a m of the United States, initiated its own program of participant training. In the subsequent years, there has been a pattern of continuing growth in the number of participants AID and its predecessor agencies have brought to the United States. The number of community development participants has increased as well. In 1964 alone, 119 community development participants were brought to the United States to study. T h e r e were thirty-six from Africa, nineteen from the Far East, sixty from Latin America, and four from the Near East. This compares with the forty-seven who were brought in 1956. [2]

In the early years of the history of United States involvement in overseas programs of community development, there was considerable opposition among the staff to training community development participants in t h e United States. However, the popularity of participant training within AID, and especially a predecessor agency, ICA, together with pressure from the developing nations to send people to the United States to study, caused a reversal of this position. As a result, by 1961, the training section within the Community Development Division of ICA had grown so large that its staff of five constituted the largest specialized arm of the division.

In spite of this growth, there are some who continue to raise questions about the value of training community development participants in the United States. They feel that frequently participants acquire knowledge, attitudes, and skills that are inappropriate for their home cultures. In addition, many participants are taught methods a n d a philosophy of community development that is different f r o m what t h e y learned in their home countries in training programs supported by the United States.

On the other hand, those defending participant training

in the United States argue that community development is part of the American tradition and a recognizable part of the American way of life. Many of the goals the new nations set for themselves are working realities in America. Notable among these goals are: self-reliance, self-help, mutual support, group activity, civic consciousness, civic responsibility, and civic pride. Therefore, in visiting America, participants have an opportunity to observe the actual working of these principles in a functioning society.

In addition, many participants come to the United States to develop competence in teaching and in action research. Increasing competency in both these areas depends to a large degree upon intensive training in the behavioral sciences. The United States provides resources and opportunities for study in most of the behavioral sciences that cannot be equaled anywhere else in the world.

It is difficult to generalize about the participants who study in the United States because the backgrounds of the participants change from year to year. For instance, from 1955 to 1958, there was a shift in the major source of origin of the participants from Europe to the Near East, South Asia, and the Far East. There was an increase in the average duration of their training programs from 3.1 months in 1955 to 10.1 months in 1958. Their average age dropped, and the number reporting postgraduate study diminished.[3] Changes of this type render it difficult to make anything but broad generalizations about participants who study in the United States.

However, there is one aspect which has remained fairly constant throughout these changes; and that is the framework of the training resources the United States provides for participants in the field of community development. These resources fall into three different, but interrelated, categories. They include academic training, field observation, and visits to government agencies and professional organizations.

THE ROLE OF COLLEGES AND UNIVERSITIES IN CROSS-CULTURAL TRAINING IN COMMUNITY DEVELOPMENT

AID and its predecessor agencies have made extensive use of United States universities and colleges in developing programs to train community development participants. Seminars, conferences with leading scholars in all fields, and regular course work are provided in all parts of the country. Currently, the most active institutions are the University of California, Berkeley; the University of Missouri; Cornell University; Michigan State University; and the University of Wisconsin.

Unfortunately, there are a limited number of American colleges and universities that have programs that are adequate for the needs of participants. This is due largely to the difference between the way many United States academicians look at community development and the way it is viewed by those in developing nations. While there is general agreement on the importance of the self-help principle and the significance of democratic values and processes, there is a wide range of difference in the emphasis placed upon such procedural concepts as the multipurpose worker and national support.

The concept of the multipurpose worker is not as widely supported in the United States as it is in the developing nations. At most universities, community workers are trained in only one area: health, education, agriculture, or home economics, but rarely in a combination of areas. A number of the colleges that train community workers operate on a principle that is markedly similar to the traditional "community school" concept, except that they look upon the college rather than the elementary school as the center of community reform. [4] This approach is not effective in solving the problems of communities whose problems are rooted in national difficulties, nor is it accepted by countries, such as India and the Philippines, who want to achieve sweeping national reforms. Obviously, training programs based upon the assumption that community reform can be achieved by a handful of colleges have limited value for participants who return to countries that have national community development programs.

In addition to the inappropriateness of the concepts taught, universities and colleges use poor techniques of instruction. Strong emphasis is placed upon the lecture method. On occasion, there are attempts to solve this problem by scheduling seminars. However, the seminars often develop into lecture sessions for smaller groups.

This problem is intensified by the preference among many instructors for the theoretical to the virtual exclusion of the practical. In many of the institutions where practical work has been attempted, the efforts reflect Americal cultural patterns that a r e not always relevant to the needs of students from developing nations. In too many college programs the backgrounds of the students are not taken into account, the teaching pace is too fast for their rate of absorption, and almost no provision is made for recall, reinforcement, association, or integration of new learning. These shortcomings violate the most elemental educational principles and tend to reinforce patterns of behavior in students from abroad that lessen their effectiveness as community development workers when they return home.

Another major problem faced by some participants in American colleges and universities is the inadequacy of faculty counseling. In many cases, the participants find themselves adrift on the college campus with little provision for help from people who are familiar with their backgrounds and their needs. The pressures placed upon American college and university professors to do research, writing, and to engage in community activities leave them with very little time to build close personal relations with either American or foreign students.

However, the picture is not entirely negative. There are many ideas the participants take away from a protracted experience in almost any American university that are valuable. Certainly one such learning is the role the university can play in community development programs. Participants observe firsthand that the universities can strengthen existing community programs through research, evaluation, consultation, the administration of pilot programs, experiments in the behavioral sciences, and course offerings in fields related to community development.

Only a few universities and colleges in developing countries have had, at one time or another, activities that are directly related to community development--notably Puerto Rico, Lebanon, and India. On the other hand, there are numerous universities in the United States that engage in all of these activities. Their activities provide a timely lesson for the participants on the role the university can play in community development programs.

Also, every community development program requires specialists. They are needed in local government, communications skills, research methods, and staff development and training. Whatever the area, specialists have to receive intensive training in an academic subject or in a professional skill before they can render assistance. The university is a very good place for education of this type. This, then, constitutes another positive r o l e a large number of American universities can play in the training of participants.

Over the years, AID and its predecessor agencies have attempted to create improved educational facilities for participants. In doing so, they have had a positive effect upon the over-all quality of community development training programs in the United States. The major contribution has been the support given to the new type of community development training programs at the University of California, Berkeley, and the University of Missouri, Columbia.

The Berkeley program, initiated in 1959, represents an attempt to coordinate the fields of rural sociology, cultural anthropology, extension methods, community development, adult education, public administration, social psychology and group dynamics, health a n d sanitation, and social welfare. The first program, which included field trips in the United States, Puerto Rico, and Jamaica, as well as an academic program, was so successful that it was continued. [5] In constructing a program tailored to meet the needs of participants, the University of California avoided many of the limitations that characterized o t h e r training programs in the United States. The major accomplishment of the Berkeley program is the ease with which it unites the separate disciplines in the behavioral sciences around the study of community development.

The program at Berkeley, called "Principles and Practices of Community Development," is a cooperative endeavor. Faculty members from fifteen university departments have developed an integrated professional curriculum out of their common interest and experience in newly developing nations. The faculty group was brought together by Professor Paul S. Taylor, who, until his retirement from the university, was chairman of the Institute of International Studies.

The program of instruction is d e s i g n e d for officials w i t h responsibility for fostering local self-help efforts in nation-building. Participants represent both technical agencies and agencies of local and general administration. In addition to the interdisciplinary core seminar held at Berkeley, the program currently includes workshops and field observations in California, Arizona, New Mexico, Jamaica, and Puerto Rico.

THE VALUE OF FIELD OBSERVATION IN PARTICIPANT TRAINING PROGRAMS IN COMMUNITY DEVELOPMENT

A second device used by AID and its predecessor agencies in training participants is field observation. This involves planned programs of observation in communities that are assisted by one or more public agencies and in communities cooperating with colleges or universities, such as the Georgia communities active in the "College in the Country" program.

Field observation, known to some as the "whistle-stop" approach, frequently comes under fire for being an ineffectual technique in cross-cultural education. Nonetheless, it continues to occupy a great proportion of the training time of participants in the United States.

Very few would argue against the principle that the more senses a person uses, the greater the possibility for learning. Certainly, the old Chinese proverb, "One picture is worth a thousand words," indicates that this principle has been supported for centuries. However, the implementation of the principle in field observation programs is as difficult to achieve as the principle itself is easy to accept.

There are a number of reasons for this. First, the development of acute observational skills in any one area requires special training. This is true whether the field is microbiology or community development. Highly developed observational skills in one field in no way guarantees observational skills in other areas. Lawyers, doctors, educators, and anthropologists are all trained to be highly observant in their own fields; yet this does not mean they are equally adept at observation in other fields. Therefore, the success of field trips depends upon the participant's skill in observing community development programs out in the field. Without this skill, the observation trips can become no more than a hodgepodge of disconnected and meaningless visual experiences.

Also, many participants find that the pace of their trips is so fast that they become exhausted very early in their programs. At times, so many visits are scheduled that the participants no sooner adjust to one situation than they are moved on to another. The experience of so many changes in food, language, clothing, and climate renders it almost impossible for them to concentrate on anything but these changes. Actually, community development participants, especially those from the Philippines, are more fortunate than most in terms of personal comfort during their travels. This is due to AID staff members, such as Barbara Doyle, who have a strong commitment to community development as a world movement and, thus, make every effort to plan meaningful trips for participants in this area.

Often these difficulties are due to the absence of specific educational objectives for bringing participants to the United States in the first place and to the failure to define clear training objectives after they arrive. This necessarily results in a situation in which no one really is able to explain why the participants visit the places they do or how their visits relate to the work they will do when they return home.

However, the case for field observation is not hopeless. There are many ways in which these deficiencies can be corrected. Participants should be given an extensive training course in observation techniques before they are sent into the field. The length of time they spend in any one place should be lengthened, and the total number of visits should be lessened. A group leader should be assigned to each group of participants to provide an element of continuity throughout the program and to arrange for periods of recall, reinforcement, and explanation.

In addition, emphasis should be changed from a program of field observation to field work. A seeing experience is not nearly as educational as a doing experience. The programs tend to operate entirely on the spectator level. The chances for participant learning can be increased considerably if the participants are given more opportunity to participate in the programs they observe. This can be attained through an internship or an on-the-job training program in which the participant is apprenticed to a skilled counterpart.

If these steps are taken, the traveling classroom concept

will replace the "whistle-stop" approach;and the importance of
field observation as an educational enterprise will be re-
established. A change of this nature requires more preplan-
ning of visits, the relating of the visits to the participant's
background, needs, and culture, and an integrated training
program. The latter objective calls for the coordination of
the participant's training in his home country before he leaves
and after he returns with the training he receives in the
United States. This can be accomplished through a predepar-
ture training program to ease his cultural adjustment to the
United States and additional training in the form of yearly
conferences, news bulletins, and annual reports after he returns to his home country.

In spite of its many shortcomings, field observation has
great potential as a learning device in the field of community
development. However, for this potential to be realized,
planners have to regard it as an educational activity and must
make every effort to operate field observation programs within the framework of sound educational principles and techniques. This means the programs have to be planned from
the same perspective and with the same painstaking care that
a teacher is expected to exercise in preparing for his classes.

THE USE OF GOVERNMENT AGENCIES AND PROFESSIONAL
ORGANIZATIONS IN PARTICIPANT TRAINING PROGRAMS

Another resource used in the participant training programs supported by AID and its predecessor agencies has
been the use of government agencies and professional organizations. The government agencies used are the Departments
of the Interior; Health, Education and Welfare; Agriculture;
Labor; and the Bureau of the Census. Also used are professional organizations, such as the Council on Social Work
Education and the Rural Sociology Society.[6] Although the
United States does not have a separate department for the administration of community development programs comparable
to those India and the Philippines have, it does provide numerous technical services on the national level. The study of
some of these services is of value to participants as is the
study of voluntary organizations which can provide participants with an insight into the role citizens' groups play in a
democratic society.

There are a number of problems related to this type of

training. Many of the professional organizations are not staffed to handle visitors from other lands nor are they fully oriented to the international scene. True, there are exceptions; but visits to these organizations by participants are generally unsatisfactory.

The word "participant" should be taken for what it means, and participation should be regarded as the key concept. However, in most visits, the participant is "talked to. " As a result, visits to government agencies and professional organizations have all the disadvantages of the poorest type of field observation program, plus the added disadvantage of containing no provision for the actual observation of a program in operation. These visits are frequently described as consultation. Even in this area, they fall far short of the ideal.

What is so often passed off as participant training is no more than participant travel, and even this is done poorly. Many of the participants, while visiting government agencies and professional organizations, find themselves traveling around alone and unattended. While they are treated courteously during office hours, they are frequently neglected in the evenings and over the weekends.

Professional organizations entertain so many visitors each day that they are unable to give the participants more than passing attention. Visits with government officials rarely, if ever, lead to personal invitations for after-office-hours meetings. As a result, the cultural adjustment is much more difficult than it would otherwise be; and the educational value of participants' visits is diminished.

THIRD-COUNTRY TRAINING

The training the United States provides outside the United States in a nation other than the participant's own is called third-country training. This type of training is a co-operative venture between the United States, the participant's home country, and the country where the training is conducted.

A significant portion of United States sponsored participant training programs are conducted in third countries. In 1965, a total of sixty-four participants in the field of community development were trained exclusively in third countries by the United States. More than half of these participants were trained in Taiwan and the Philippines. In addition, there are a large number of participants who are trained in both the United States and a third country. The countries currently used for combined United States and third-country training include Israel, Taiwan, Korea, Jamaica, India, the Philippines, and Pakistan.

Third-country training is particularly valuable for participants representing countries that are newly independent and just inaugurating a community development program. The opportunity to study in a nation not too much further advanced than their own seems to make much more sense than studying in one of the more advanced nations. Many of the leaders of developing nations look more favorably upon third-country participant training than they do upon training in the United States. They feel that third-country training is less of a threat to their policy of neutrality and nonalignment than training in the United States is. In addition, they feel that cultural adjustment is easier for their participants in another developing nation than it is in the United States. Politically, the developing nations also recognize the value in interchanging participants among themselves as a means of strengthening their bonds of unity and friendship.

However, third-country training presents problems. Most of the countries used for third-country training are not equipped to train large numbers of nationals from other countries. Taiwan and the Philippines share the largest number of participants trained in third countries by the United States. Yet, both countries have to struggle merely to meet the demands of training their own people with limited resources.

Robert Polson reports that the Philippines finds itself overburdened with third-country trainees and observers from other countries. He says that it is a relatively small country with limited facilities for training large numbers of visitors. One immediate solution, he suggests, is the selection of fewer participants for a training program especially designed for third-country participants.[7]

The major difficulty in developing sound third-country training programs is the scarcity of information on the training facilities of countries outside Europe. An excellent survey has been published on the training facilities for community development participants in Europe. However, there is no study as of now of the opportunities and facilities for training in Asia and Africa.

THE UTILIZATION OF TRAINING

One question invariably asked by those concerned with participant training deals with the extent to which participants trained by the United States utilize their training when they return home. Although there are a number of studies directed specifically to this question, none of them provides a fully satisfactory answer.

Some critics feel that the training most participants receive is so inappropriate that it is virtually impossible for them to utilize it at home. Others believe that it is unrealistic to expect that a nation's development can be significantly pushed forward by a few individuals trained abroad. This latter group feels that change is brought about through institutions. Therefore, they feel that those who are capable of changing national institutions should be trained within the framework of the institutions they are expected to change. They believe further that participants trained in the United States and third countries cannot implement their training in their home countries unless their training is part of a country-wide plan to change institutions.

Clearly, the question of how well participants utilize their training is still an open one in 1967 and requires much more research before it can be answered.

CONCLUSION

Obviously, participant training is one of international education's biggest problem areas. Yet, it continues to be neglected as a proper subject for serious study by educationists and noneducationists alike. This neglect has hampered significant progress in the field. Nonetheless, there are a number of common-sense principles that have emerged as experience in participant training has grown.

First, training programs should be carefully planned in the light of the needs of the participants' countries. Participants should not be brought to the United States or a third country merely to meet quotas. Their training should be based upon clear-cut and measurable objectives.

Second, criteria for the selection of participants to study in the United States or a third country should be carefully defined. It is grossly unfair to the student, the country he represents, and the United States to select participants who cannot benefit from their training because of inadequate qualifications. A good training program, no matter how highly rated, is valueless if the participants are not competent enough to benefit from it.

Third, participants should be given careful and intelligent advice throughout their training. This should be built into every training program from the very beginning. Participants, in pursuing studies, operate in a new culture and under pressure conditions. They are constantly in need of informed advice on the way to use their time and their talents most effectively.

Finally, steps should be taken to help the participants implement their training when they return to their home countries. This final phase should be considered an important part of the over-all training program. The real test of the success of the advanced training is the participants' success in implementing their new learnings in their own nations. [8]

NOTES TO CHAPTER 7

[1]United States ICA, Office of Participant Training, Participant Training Operations (Washington, D.C.: ICA, 1960), Introduction.

[2]Ibid., p. 8.

[3]United States ICA, Community Development Division, "An Analysis of ICA Training Programs in the United States for Participants in Community Development" (Washington, D.C.: The Division, ICA, 1959), p. 3.

[4]William W. Biddle, A Pattern of Fundamental Education, Earlham College Bulletin, New Series 38, No. 2 (Richmond, Ind.: Earlham College, Winter, 1955-56), p. 22.

[5]"Community Stability for New Nations," California Monthly, LXXI (December, 1960), 4-10.

[6]United States ICA, "Analysis," op. cit., p. 9.

[7]Robert A. Polson, "A Report on the Training Aspects of the Philippine Community Development Program" (Manila: ICA, 1960), p. 29.

[8]The Carnegie Foundation for the Advancement of Teaching, The College and the University in International Affairs (New York: The Foundation, n. d.), p. 9.

CHAPTER **8** SUMMARY

Numerous studies have been undertaken on economic, political, and cultural implications of intergovernmental programs in community development. However, the study of the role of education in these programs has been largely neglected. The central purpose of this book is to analyze the philosophy, the functions, and the operations of United States technical assistance activities in the field of community development in order to discover the role education plays in intergovernmental programs in community development.

Organizationally, the book is divided into two parts. The first part deals with the philosophy, the functions, and the operations of the United States community development staff overseas. The second part is an analysis of community development as an educational process, a description of the training programs, and a discussion of the educational aspects of advisory assistance.

The book is based upon a number of assumptions. The first is that the work of United States community development personnel overseas is an integral and an effective part of the technical cooperation programs of AID. The second is that community development is an educational process. And the third is that advisory assistance and training programs for community development workers in their home countries and abroad are key elements in strong intergovernmental programs in community development.

The principle development tools of AID are defined as development loans, development grants and technical cooperation, supporting assistance, and the contingency fund. Of these, the most relevant to community development is technical cooperation.

Although the United States engaged in a few technical cooperation programs with less-developed nations before 1945, there is almost no precedent in United States history for the

114

scope or the kind of programs AID and its predecessor agencies undertook in subsequent years. The earliest programs the United States was involved in do not go back much before the creation of the Institute of American Affairs in 1938. Between 1938 and 1961, when AID was established, the governmental agencies that conducted the technical cooperation program were named the Technical Cooperation Administration, the Economic Cooperation Administration, the Mutual Security Administration, and the International Cooperation Administration.

The discussion of the functions of AID is followed by an examination of some of the major bench marks in the history of United States technical assistance activities in the field of community development overseas. These are the support given to India and Pakistan to undertake national community development programs in 1952, the creation of a separate division for community development within the United States Government in 1954, the publication of "The Community Development Guidelines of the International Cooperation Administration" in 1956, which outlined a basic philosophy, and the agreement to support the Philippine Community Development Program that was signed in 1956.

Each of these activities has played an important role in the philosophy of community development formulated by the United States for its overseas programs. Because of these experiences, the United States places strong emphasis upon national support, intensive training programs for all levels of personnel, the use of the multipurpose worker on the village level, the self-help principle, and political objectives in all the nations it assists.

Although the community development staff supports an assistance philosophy which is quite distinct from that held by staff members in other technical areas within AID, it shares the same functions. The functions are advisory assistance, the exchange of information, training, and the provision of small amounts of material assistance and dollar aid.

The United States has made a number of contributions to the growth of community development programs around the world. First, it supported community development as a means of overcoming social and economic problems at a time when the leaders of developing nations were searching for a concept upon which to build programs of sweeping national reform.   Second, it has played a vital role in synthesizing the many scattered ideas on community development into a unified concept.   Third, it has helped establish community development as an important international movement.   And, fourth, it has demonstrated the effectiveness of community development as a means of eradicating tyranny, hunger, and disease.

The second half of the book deals with the role of international education in intergovernmental programs in community development.   This calls for a new way of looking at the relationship between education and community development.

Traditionally, the role of education in community development has been thought of in terms of literacy training, the community school concept, and fundamental education.   This study reveals that, at least in intergovernmental programs in community development, the role is much broader.   United States community development staff members function nationally and internationally as well as on the level of village-type communities.   Their activities represent joint enterprises carried on by individuals from greatly divergent cultures and, therefore, are much different from those conducted by a single nation at home.

For this reason, new educational functions and forms have emerged.   These are evidenced in the work of the community development adviser, national training programs for community development personnel, and participant training in the United States and third countries.

Advisory assistance, as a component of technical cooperation, generally is characterized by a voluntary agreement in which an outside adviser enters into a temporary relationship with the representatives of another country in order to help them solve their existing problems through professional assistance.

The adviser is expected to identify the key people in the group he is advising, to establish a satisfactory working relationship with them, and to help them clarify their problems and to select appropriate solutions.   In addition, he has to teach them the procedures and the skills necessary for achieving the goals he has helped them set.

There is no clear-cut agreement upon the exact dimensions of the adviser's role. One group of advisers believe that, once they identify the problems of the group they are called to assist, their next task is to correct the problems for the group. Advisers who support this point of view are called "practitioners."

Another group of advisers see themselves as consultants and no more. Once they identify and diagnose a group's problems, they p r e p a r e a set of recommendations for the group to follow.

A third group, and by far the largest, look upon themselves as consultant-trainers. These advisers add the function of training to the basic functions of identifying the problems, making a diagnosis, and preparing recommendations. A number of advisers in this category also add institution-building to their other functions.

The role of education in advisory assistance is best demonstrated among the advisers who think of themselves as consultant-trainers. For them, the very process of giving advice is educational; and they consider training to be a major element in the adviser's work. They feel that advisers should be selected on the basis of their ability to educate as well as on their technical competence. Also, they place great value upon training in the use of audio-v i s u a l aids and g r o u p dynamics and the ability to write and to speak in layman terms about their own technical fields.

A second major educational task carried on by the United States community development staff overseas is the development of f o r m a l and systematic training programs f o r all community development workers throughout their entire careers. In the implementation of this objective, the staff supports p r e s e r v i c e, in-service, orientation, and refresher courses for administrators, technicians, multipurpose village-level workers, and local leaders.

The community development staff gives particular attention to the training programs for multipurpose workers. In these training programs, the staff stresses the need for building human relations skills and technical proficiency, emphasis upon the practical rather than the academic, and the active participation of the trainees in the learning experience.

The staff also stresses the need for selecting village workers on the basis of previous village experience and facility in the language of the region where they are to work. It emphasizes, as well, that the trainees' initial training program be supplemented with periodic in-service courses.

In spite of the efforts of the United States, there are many shortcomings in the community development training programs of most of the aided countries. Frequently, those running the programs ignore sound educational principles and are careless in their selection procedures. In addition, in many of the programs, there is a wide gap between the theory taught in the classroom and the work the trainees have to do in the field.

A third educational task the United States supports is participant training in the United States and third countries. Many educators question the value of training community development workers from other countries in the United States. Nonetheless, the United States, over the years, has intensified its participant training activities to such a point that, numerically, subject-fieldwise, and geographically, it has built a program unparalleled in history.

The United States supports three types of participant training. These are academic training, field observation, and the visitation of governmental and professional organizations. None of these approaches is totally satisfactory.
This is partly because those in the institutions the participants visit often support a concept of community development that differs from the one the United States believes to be most appropriate for developing nations. Also, many of the participants receive insufficient guidance.

Another form of participant training is third-country training. Many of the leaders of neutral nations favor this approach because it fits into their policies of neutrality more easily than training in the United States does. However, third-country training also has its limitations. The countries where this training should be conducted rarely have the training resources to do an adequate job.

Socially, politically, and economically, technical assistance is an important way for nations of better means to meet their obligations to those of lesser means. Unfortunately, the amount of technical assistance that any nation can give is, of necessity, small. However, the impact of even a small amount of aid can be increased if those working in international programs understand the processes which underlie technical assistance, especially as these processes relate to advisory assistance and the training of nationals at home and abroad.

Although the focus of this book is upon the community development activities of AID and its predecessor agencies, many of the questions under discussion can just as well be applied to the technical assistance programs undertaken in agriculture, health, labor, or public administration.

The fundamental processes involved in technical assistance are fairly consistent from field to field. True, the products differ; but, more often than not, the factors that spell success are the same. In this sense, this book is more than an analysis of international education and community development. In many ways, it is a much broader study of the role of technical cooperation in the development of new nations.

BIBLIOGRAPHY

Books

Batten, T.R. Communities and Their Development. London:
   Oxford University Press, 1957. Pp. 248.

_____. Training for Community Development: A Critical Study
   of Method. London: Oxford University Press, 1962. Pp. 192.

Biddle, William and Loureide J. Biddle. The Community Development Process: The Rediscovery of Local Initiative. New York:
   Holt, Rinehart and Winston, Inc., 1965. Pp. 334.

Dey, S.K. Community Development. Delhi: Kitab Mahal, 1960.
   Pp. 199.

Dube, S.C. India's Changing Villages: Human Factors in Community
   Development. Ithaca, New York: Cornell University Press,
   1958. Pp. 230.

Dunham, Arthur. Community Welfare Organization: Principles and
   Practice. New York: Crowell, 1958. Pp. 480.

du Sautoy, Peter. Community Development in Ghana. London:
   Oxford University Press, 1958. Pp. 209.

_____. The Organization of A Community Development Programme.
   London: Oxford University Press, 1962. Pp. 156.

Foster, George M. Traditional Cultures: and the Impact of Techno-
   logical Change. New York: Harper and Brothers, 1962. Pp. 292.

Hayden, Howard. Moturiki: A Pilot Project in Community Development.
   London: Oxford University Press, 1954. Pp. 180.

King, Clarence. Working With People in Community Action. New
   York: Association Press, 1965. Pp. 192.

121

_____. Working With People in Small Communities : Case Records of Community Development in Different Countries. New York: Harper and Brothers, 1958. Pp. 130.

Mayer, Albert, et al. Community Project, India. Berkeley, California: University of California Press, 1958. Pp. 367.

Mezirow, Jack D. Dynamics of Community Development. New York: The Scarecrow Press, 1963. Pp. 252.

Mukerji, B. Community Development in India. Bombay: Orient Longmans, 1961. Pp. 312.

Ogden, Jean and Jess Ogden. Small Communities in Action: Stories of Citizen Programmes at Work. New York: Harper and Brothers, 1946. Pp. 244.

_____. These Things We Tried. Charlottesville: The University of Virginia, 1947. Pp. 432.

Poston, Richard W. Democracy Speaks Many Tongues: Community Development Around the World. New York: Harper and Row, 1962. Pp. 206.

Ross, Murray G. Case Histories in Community Organization. New York: Harper and Brothers, 1958. Pp. 259.

_____. Community Organization: Theory and Principles. New York: Harper and Brothers, 1955. Pp. 128.

Ruopp, Phillipps (ed.). Approaches to Community Development. The Hague: W. Van Hoeve, 1953 . Pp. 352.

Wiser, Charlotte V. and William H. Wiser. Behind Mud Walls 1930-1960. Berkeley and Los Angeles: University of California Press, 1964. Pp. 249.

Periodicals and Yearbooks

Adams, Lucy W. "Urban Community Development: Its Role in Developing Societies." Community Development Review, VIII (March, 1963), 27-29.

Buitron, Anibal. "Community Development in Theory and Practice,"
Community Development Review, VI (September, 1961), 14-21.

Cousins, William J. "Community Development in West Bengal."
Community Development Review, IV (September, 1959), 37-77.

Dube, S.C. "Some Problems of Communication in Rural Community
Development." Economic Development and Cultural Change,
V (1957), 129-46.

Dunham, Arthur. "Adventure in Education--An Experimental Seminar
in Community Development." Community Development Bulletin,
X (December, 1958), 7-13.

_____. "The Outlook for Community Development: An International
Symposium." International Review of Community Development,
V (1960), 33-50.

Ensminger, Douglas. "Community Development and Its Contributions
to National Development." Community Development Review, VI
(June, 1961), 10-16.

Foster, George M. "Guidelines to Community Development Programs."
Community Development Bulletin, VIII (March, 1957), 34-38.

Gales, Edwin A. "Political Implications of Community Development
Programs in the Newly Developing Areas of the World."
Community Development Review, VI (September, 1961), 4-13.

Goswami, U.L. "Three Facets of Community Development."
Community Development Bulletin, I (January, 1956), 12-19.

Gray, Jack D. "Training for Community Development." Community
Development Bulletin, II (September, 1956), 44-51.

Green, James W. "Community Development as Economic Development: The Role of Value Orientation." Community Development
Review, V (September, 1960), 1-24.

_____. "Rural Community Development in Pakistan: The Village
A.I.D. Program." Community Development Review, VI
(September, 1957), 45-69.

Kelly, Isabel. "Suggestions for the Training of Village Level Workers." Community Development Review, VIII (June, 1963), 89-94.

Langley, Grace E. "Community Development Programme, Republic of India." Community Development Review, VI (September, 1957), 6-23.

Mezirow, Jack D. "Community Development Extension and Village Aid Synthesis." Community Development Information, II (January-February, 1961), 6-13.

_____. "Community Development as an Educational Process." International Review of Community Development, V (1960), 137-50.

Mial, H.D. and D. Mial. "The Development, Training, and Use of Leadership Resources in Community Development Programs." Community Development Review, VII (June, 1962), 21-28.

Miniclier, Louis M. "Community Development Defined." Community Development Review, III (December, 1956), 1-2.

_____. "Economic Development and Community Development." Community Development Review, VIII (June, 1963), 25-29.

_____. "Social Group Work in Community Development Programs." Community Organization 1960. New York: Columbia University Press, 1960. Pp. 117-27.

_____. "Values and Principles of Community Development." International Review of Community Development, V (1960), 57-61.

Neal, Ernest E. "Community Development in the Philippines." Community Development Review, VI (September, 1957), 24-44.

_____. "The Role of the Community Development Advisor." Community Development Bulletin, II (September, 1956), 54-61.

Neff, Kenneth L. "Education and The Forces of Change." International Development Review, IV (March, 1962), 22-25.

Niederfrank, E.J. and Lucy Wellborn Cole. "Education for Community Development." Review of Educational Research, XXIX (June, 1959), 304-7.

Perpetua, Antonio. "Community Development As a New Institution of Government." Community Development Review, VI (June, 1961), 17-33.

Polson, Robert A. "Theory and Methods of Training for Community Development." Rural Sociology, XXIII (March, 1958), 34-42.

Rose, Paul W. "Community Mobilization: The Way of Free Men to Mobilize Their Resources for Development and Democracy." Community Development Review, VIII (March, 1963), 37-41.

Sanders, Irwin T. "Theories of Community Development." Rural Sociology, XXIII (March, 1958), 1-12.

Solomon, Darwin. "An Approach to Training for Community Development." International Review of Community Development, III (1959), 25-33.

Taylor, Carl C. "Community Development Programs and Methods." Community Development Review, III (December, 1956), 34-42.

Turner, J. Sheldon. "Capacity for Self-Growth Through Community Development." Community Development Review, VIII (June, 1963), 95-99.

Verner, Coolie. "The Community Development Process." Community Development Review, VI (March, 1961), 49-58.

Witte, Ernest F. "Community Development in Selected Countries." Community Development Review, VII (June, 1962), 1-10.

Publications of Governments, Learned Societies, and Other Organizations

Adams, Harold S., George M. Foster, and Paul S. Taylor. Report on Community Development Programs in India, Pakistan and the Philippines. Washington, D.C.: ICA, 1955. Pp. 88.

Ensminger, Douglas. A Guide to Community Development. Delhi, India: The Ministry of Community Development, 1957. Pp. 205.

Gibson, William C., Hugh B. Masters, and Ernest F. Witte. Community Development Programs in India, Iran, Egypt and the Gold Coast. Washington, D.C.: ICA, 1955. Pp. 101.

Mezirow, Jack D. The Literature on Community Development: A Bibliographic Guide. Washington, D.C.: AID and The Peace Corps, n.d. Pp. 177.

_____, and Frank A. Santopolo. "Five Years of Community Development in Pakistan." Village Aid. Lahore, West Pakistan: Village Aid Administration, 1960. Pp. 206.

Milburn, S. Methods and Techniques of Community Development in the United Kingdom Dependent and Trust Territories. New York: United Nations, 1954. Pp. 111.

Neal, Ernest. A Report to the Assistant Administrator for Technical Cooperation Research on the Agency for International Development Program of Community Development Assistance. Washington, D.C.: AID, 1964. Pp. 65.

Philippines, Office of the President. Training and the Community Development Center. Manila: Office of the President, n.d. Pp. 15.

Sanders, Irwin T. Community Development and National Change. Washington, D.C.: Community Development Division, ICA, 1958. Pp. 70.

Taylor, Carl C. A Critical Analysis of India's Community Development Program. India: Community Projects Administration, 1956. Pp. 62.

Thomson, R. Educational Aspects of Community Development. South Pacific Commission Technical Paper No. 74. Norumea, New Caledonia: South Pacific Commission, 1955. Pp. 89.

United Kingdom, Colonial Office. Community Development--A Handbook. London: Her Majesty's Stationery Office, 1958. Pp. 34.

United Nations. Study Kit on Training for Community Development. New York: United Nations, 1957. Pp. 69.

United Nations, Bureau of Social Affairs. Social Progress Through Community Development. New York: United Nations, 1955. Pp. 120.

United States AID. "Community Development and Social Change."
     Community Development. Series A. Volume 4. Washington,
     D. C. : AID, 1962. Pp. 16.

_____. "Community Development, Extension and The Village AID
     Synthesis." Community Development. Series A. Volume 5.
     Washington, D. C. : AID, 1962. Pp. 12.

_____. "CD in Urban and Semi-Urban Areas." Community
     Development. Series A. Volume 3. Washington, D. C. : AID,
     1962. Pp. 20.

_____. "An Introduction to CD For Village Workers." Community
     Development. Series A. Volume 1. Washington , D. C. : AID,
     1962. Pp. 27.

_____. Principles of Foreign Economic Assistance. Washington,
     D. C. : AID, 1965 (Revised). Pp. 52.

_____. "The Village-AID Worker and Democratic Program Planning."
     Community Development. Series A. Volume 7. Washington,
     D. C. : AID, 1962. Pp. 32.

_____. Office of Technical Cooperation and Research. Community
     Development Abstracts. Washington, D. C. : AID, n. d. Pp. 281.

United States Department of Health, Education and Welfare, Office of
     Education. Education for Better Living. Washington, D. C. :
     Government Printing Office, 1957. Pp. 339.

United States Department of State. ICA What It Is, What It Does.
     Washington, D. C. : Government Printing Office, 1959. Pp. 13.

ABOUT THE AUTHOR

James J. Shields, Jr. has served as a consultant on education and world affairs to a number of national organizations and has lectured widely on African education. In 1961-62, he served as a researcher in East Africa where he studied the effectiveness of 150 young American teachers who were brought there in a program financed by the U.S. Agency for International Development.

He has written a number of monographs and has had articles published in The Yearbook of Education, The Comparative Education Review, The Pennsylvania School Journal, and The International Development Review. He is also co-author of Problems and Prospects in International Education, soon to be published.

Dr. Shields is Assistant Professor on the faculty of City College, the City University of New York, and has also taught at the State University College, New Paltz, New York; Queens College; and Columbia University. For the last three years, he has been a visiting lecturer at Teachers College, Columbia University, where he has given a course in international education.